MICKEY: SURVIVING SALVATION

ROBERT "MICKEY" SHAFER

RUNNING WILD

This book is dedicated to all of the underdogs, who have to fight for their way through life.

CHAPTER ONE

My name is Mickey. I'm the middle of five brothers and the only blond in my family. At my birth in Chicago, Illinois in 1942, Dad declared me a bastard and cruelly nick-named me Blondie. Luckily, he abandoned my mom Virginia and our family when I turned five-years-old. The bad part was he took my youngest brother, eighteen-month-old John, with him to California. Most of the time I didn't miss the mean bully, but I was really sad he took my baby brother and made Mom cry so much.

Two years later, when I was seven-years-old, Mom allowed my other younger brother, five-year-old Steve, to be adopted by a woman who wanted a companion for her own four-year-old son. Mom placed a want ad in a Chicago newspaper looking for a home for Ken, Steve and I. We three brothers made an overnight visit to the woman's house. Doris decided she wanted to keep Steve, but not Ken and I. I guess she took Steve because he was the youngest and got along better with her whiny kid than Ken or I did.

Right after, Mom gave me to a well-meaning older couple

from Lisle who answered the same advertisement. It really hurt when she left me with strangers. I cried more than I believed possible. But, a year later, smiling and glamorous Mom showed up for a Christmas visit. Those nice people, Rose and George, wanted to adopt me, but Mom refused and she lovingly reclaimed me. Mom promised she and I'd be together forever. She wouldn't say if I'd ever see my two younger brothers again.

In 1951, after I spent another year rampaging on the streets of Chicago with my two older brothers and I had turned nine-years-old, my mother found a new home for me by posting another advertisement in a Chicago newspaper. The woman she gave me to was the biggest and scariest person I'd ever been left alone with. Naomi angered quickly and beat me without mercy. She forced me to be her house-slave and shoplifting expert. The monster made me her prisoner.

I lived in bondage to Naomi for four terrible years before I became brave enough to run away. The coppers who caught me didn't believe one word I said and returned me to her. Before the big-fisted brute could climb up to my room and beat me to death, she suffered a stroke and went into a coma. A few months later, she died.

I attended the beast's funeral and watched six-feet of black, wormy earth being shoveled onto the top of her fancy casket. My good luck again. I always feared she'd kill me during one of her violent rages.

Naomi's widower, Emil, who always ignored my existence, found a younger woman to replace Naomi. Neither of them wanted me around, so he tracked down my mother and told her she had to take me back. Mom said she didn't have room for me and didn't want me either, but Emil insisted.

Now, I'm on my 24-hour train trip from Chicago, Illinois to Ogden, Utah to be reunited with my mom, Virginia. I barely remember her. I'm terrified.

CHAPTER TWO

After four years of abandonment, I'm returning to my mother. Again.

I rubbed my shirtsleeve across my runny nose. My oversized clothes gave me plenty of cloth to wipe away the snot. I steadied myself as the creaking and clattering Union Pacific Overland stretched out to its full length and rolled out of Chicago's Union Station. It was six o'clock in the evening in the year 1954. I was twelve-years-old and my life wasn't showing a lot of promise. I told myself I didn't care about anybody or anything, but like a sissy, I cried a few tears when Emil walked away and I was alone in the world.

Making a train trip was exciting, but riding these rails to the unknown scared me. My mother, who didn't want me returned to her, and her new husband, awaited my arrival in Ogden, Utah. A new man for Virginia always meant trouble for her sons before. There'd be bullying and threats of beatings, but the getting-rid-of talk was always the worst part.

I could still hear the men from the past.

"Your boys are nothing but trouble, Virginia."

"I love you, Virginia, but I can't tolerate your sons."

"You should find their father and make him take care of his own damn kids."

Four years since Mom abandoned me and I hadn't heard one word from her until two weeks ago. I knew nothing about her new husband.

I tried to forget about all the bad stuff in my life.

"They can all go to hell," I muttered to myself. "I have my own train window to look out. Right now, I'm free and having fun."

I watched Chicago's tall buildings and sparkling downtown lights grow distant and dim. We rolled past a blur of low wood and brick structures with dirty smoke drifting from chimneys. Eventually, occasional blinking neon signs were the only hint of human existence. The train picked up speed. I leaned back in my seat and closed my eyes.

Naomi's angry face suddenly appeared and hovered over me. She raised her big fist and swung at me. I barely dodged her punch to my face.

I opened my eyes. Damn the blackness. I wasn't going to find refuge there. I needed to find a way to erase the monster from my memory. I listened to the voices of the other passengers, but I didn't want to look at anyone. I didn't want anyone to look at me. I was ashamed of my raggedy, slum boy appearance. I wished I was invisible.

I was hungry, but the jerky motions of the train made me nauseated. I couldn't face my grease-stained package of fried chicken. I shoved it as far under my seat as it would go. The neighbor lady meant well when she gave me fried chicken for my big trip, but I don't think she knew how much a train bounced around. I felt like I was on a carnival ride. Back and forth. Side to side. The damn train wouldn't quit jerking my body all over the place. I wondered how the locomotive and cars stayed on the tracks. What if we went crashing off of a high trestle bridge? I sure didn't want to be part of a deadly train wreck.

A conductor entered my car. He carried a few pillows and a couple of blankets. He was tall and wide-shouldered and his big hands made the blankets and pillows look small. Wearing a blue jacket and blue pants, a white shirt with a blue bow tie and a blue cap, he looked very much in charge of the train. Two rows of brass buttons decorated his jacket and a shiny brass insignia stood out on the front of his cap. He intimidated me as much as any copper I ran from in Chicago. He stopped and gave me a good looking over. I wasn't much to look at.

"Traveling alone, son?" he asked in a deep voice.

"Yes sir." Uh-Oh! Was something wrong? Did he forget he punched my ticket when I boarded the train? Did he think I was a dangerous stowaway who was running from the law?

"How old are you, son?"

"I'm going on thirteen, sir." He wasn't going to throw me off the train, was he?

"You look younger than twelve."

"Do you need to see my ticket again, sir?" He had me really scared.

Finally, a smile showed on his face. It wasn't a big smile, but enough to make me feel less worried. "No. I remember you now. Have a good trip, son."

"Thanks, sir." Whew. What a relief.

"Here's a blanket and pillow."

"I don't have any money, sir."

"It's okay. I won't charge you."

"Thank you, sir."

The train was only quarter full, so I had my two-passenger seat and the one across from me all to myself. I stretched out on the seat. I squeezed the soft pillow under my head and pulled the fresh-smelling blanket over myself. If my nightmares stayed away, I could sleep comfortably on this train. My empty stomach growled loudly. *Shut up stomach.* There wasn't any food to give it other than the greasy fried chicken. Toughen up, Mickey. Chicken noodle soup and saltine crackers would ease my hunger. But, there wasn't any hope for that kind of delicious and soothing meal.

Stops at stations and constantly shifting motion and loud metallic groans of the train disrupted my efforts to sleep. When I fell asleep, a nightmare pursued me.

I was back in my room at Naomi's. The big brute stood over me. She grabbed me by my hair. She swung me back and forth like a rag doll. Her big fist flew towards my face. I put my arms up to stop her from hitting me. Clawing at my hands, she screamed.

"Don't you ever fight back, you monster! Put your hands down, you filthy thug!"

I moaned. I cried. I curled in a ball. Tighter and tighter I curled until I slithered down a dark hole and fell forever. Naomi and her screaming voice faded away.

I was terribly hot and sweating. I uncurled my body. I thrashed back and forth. I struggled to stretch out fully. I forced my eyes open. It was dark. Nothing around me looked familiar. I didn't know where I was. Panic surged through me.

I recognized the clacking sound of train wheels. I saw a faint glimmer of light. I wasn't in total darkness and trapped in the terrifying solitude of a coffin like Naomi ended up. I remembered. I was aboard a train. The lights in the car were only dimmed. I was on my way out to the Wild West. I was on my way to live with my mother and her new family.

Clack.

Screech.

Groan.

The train never quit complaining. I needed to quit worrying. There was nothing for me to be afraid of anymore. Naomi was dead. She was sealed inside her fancy casket. She was buried in a deep, dark hole at the cemetery. She couldn't possibly hurt me anymore. I dozed off again.

Another nightmare, the dream that always haunted me, returned to torture me again.

I clung to the edge of the abyss. I turned my head and looked over my shoulder. Huge, dark waves rushed towards me. I lost my grip on the cliff's crumbling, dirt edge. I fell. As I fell, I turned over and over. I screamed. I grew dizzy. I fell for what seemed like forever. Suddenly, I landed in a green meadow. It was a soft landing. Above me, a brilliant blue sky glowed. In the distance, I saw and heard my two older brothers, Tommy and Ben. They were shouting and laughing to each other. They were running away from me. They grew smaller and smaller as they ran faster away from me. I attempted to stand. I desperately needed to run after them. I couldn't move. I couldn't control my legs. I yelled my loudest, "Tommy! Ben! Wait for me." My voice came out as a low rasp. My brothers didn't hear my scream for help. My brothers disappeared over the edge of the earth and I was frightfully alone. Suddenly, I was floundering on the surface of a stormy, freezing-cold ocean. The skyline was filled with gigantic dark clouds. The clouds billowed up for miles in a black, lightning streaked sky. There wasn't a moon. There weren't any stars. Suddenly, everything went black. I was under water. I was drowning.

I awoke to the semi-darkness of the train car. I heard restless sleep movements around me. I heard the breathing and snoring of other passengers. I wasn't alone. I was safe. Jesus Christ. I needed to stay awake to avoid the nightmares. But, I knew I couldn't stay awake. I couldn't stop the nightmares. Sleep always overcame me. The frightening dreams always came back to torture me.

I recovered my elusive pillow from the floor. I struggled for a comfortable position on the train seat. I lost the pillow again. I gave up on the damn thing. I pressed my head against the rough material of the seat. I heard the train wheels clicking steadily against the steel rails. The noise grew louder and drowned out all other sounds. I dozed off again.

The motion of the train became like the rocking of the cradle I spent so many hours in as a baby. Mommy leaned over me. Her smile was full of love. She brushed my hair back from my forehead. I loved the feel of her gentle hand.

"I have to leave for work now, Mickey. Be a good baby. I love you."

I cried out to her as she walked out of the room. She disappeared. Daddy's sneering face appeared above me. He looked down at me with disgust. In his finely manicured hand, he held Mommy's doll that never smiled. His face twisted into his terribly evil grin. He and the doll spoke loudly in their screechy voices. "What's wrong with you, Blondie? Why are you always crying, Blondie? Why are you always soaked in piss, Blondie? Why don't you stay in your own bed at night, Blondie?"

I screamed. Daddy and the doll cackled at me. They looked and moved like the floating witches from a scary cartoon.

The real cries, of a real live baby, broke through my terror-filled nightmare and woke me. I heard a shifting of bodies. I heard a rustling of clothes. "Here, hungry baby." A mother's soothing voice restored contentment.

Nobody came running to ask me why I screamed. It must not have happened. I was too sleepy to figure out the truth. A deep sleep enveloped me. My nightmares stayed away.

CHAPTER THREE

A lurch of the train woke me. I sat up, untangled from my blanket, and rubbed sleep from my eyes. It was morning. I was stiff and sore. I forced my eyes to focus. I saw what looked like a United States Navy sailor sitting in the seat across from me. My eyes worked better. His dark blue uniform with white striping and his black neckerchief looked genuine. He held a white sailor's hat in his hand. His brown hair was perfectly trimmed and neatly combed.

I ran my hand through my disheveled blond hair and scratched an itch on my scalp. The sailor looked at me with non-threatening curiosity. I straightened my clothes. I remembered I was on a train and I glanced out my window. The partly cloudy sky was brightening to daylight. Fields of brown stubble shivering under a thin layer of morning frost filled the flat landscape.

I turned back to see if the sailor was still there. He was. Two rows of colorful ribbons were pinned on the chest of his uniform. A red insignia of crossed flags and two red slashes decorated his left sleeve. He held his head high. He appeared to be brave and he looked confident. I thought he might be a war hero.

His warm, friendly eyes looked right at me.

Strange men of every kind scared me. When they saw me look at them, I diverted my eyes to the ground or off to the side. I always worried about men who were interested in young boys for sex. I felt safer in the world if nobody noticed me at all. I wanted to move through the world without being seen. I wanted to see everything without being seen. Many times, I wished my world was that way. I was, The Amazing Invisible Boy.

I rubbed a finger along the side of my nose. Damn itch.

I hadn't seen many wristwatches as fine as the one the sailor wore. His black shoes showed off one of the best shine jobs I ever saw. I doubted Tommy, Ben and I working together could've done a better job, and we were damn good shoeshine boys.

"Hi," he said with a strong, but kind voice. "I mean, good morning."

"Good morning, sir," I replied, unable to repress a yawn.

"You don't have to call me sir. My name is Jerry."

"Hi, Jerry," I rubbed the back of my neck and stretched my spine. Jerry wasn't nearly as intimidating as most grown-ups were.

"What's your name?" he asked.

"I'm Mickey."

"How old are you, Mickey?"

"I'm almost thirteen." I sat up taller. Jerry was easy to talk to. "How old are you, sir? I mean, Jerry."

"I'm twenty-eight." He added with pride, "I've been in the Navy for ten years, Mickey. Ten more years and I can retire. Then, I'll do another kind of work. I like to build things and work on cars. I might build race cars."

Building race cars sounded exciting. Jerry didn't seem bothered by my poor-boy appearance. His grooming was perfect and he was muscular and handsome. I thought he'd make a good actor in a war movie. All of the pretty girls would act silly over him when he returned home from bloody combat wearing lots of medals.

"Are you going to the dining car for breakfast, Mickey?"

"No sir, I mean Jerry." I pointed to the package under my seat, "I have a package of fried chicken to eat." I hoped he wasn't bothered by the smell of the greasy stuff. I sure was.

"You're going to eat fried chicken for breakfast?"

"Well, yes. I don't have any money." I sat on the edge of my seat. My right leg bobbed rapidly.

"Hmm." Jerry looked at me. I could tell he was thinking. Finally, he said, "I really like fried chicken, Mickey. I'll buy breakfast if you give me a piece later."

"Really?"

"Come on," Jerry said as he stood up. "Let's beat the rush to the dining car."

What the heck, I thought. Jerry wasn't at all like the creepy men that stared at you when you were alone and wanted to talk to you. They tried to trick you in believing they just wanted to be your friend. I usually recognized their evil intentions in their body movements and eyes. I got away from them as fast as I could.

I jumped up and followed Jerry down the aisle. He looked like he was at least six-foot- tall.

Jerry handled walking with the motion of the train much better than I did. It must have been something he learned from being on ships at sea. I saw movies where sailors struggled to keep their footing during bad storms. I grabbed onto the backs of seats as we walked down the train aisle. I pleaded with my stomach to not get upset from the constant back and forth movement of the train.

Jerry slid open the doors between the cars with ease. He was strong. My older brothers, Tommy and Ben, always laughed and left me behind to struggle with those difficult doors when we ran from car to car on the elevated trains in Chicago.

The noise level increased dramatically as Jerry and I stepped in the vestibule and corridor connector. This was one of the most fun parts of being on a train. In the movies, this is where the villain stabbed or choked to death the helpless victim, whose screams couldn't be heard above the screeching of the wheels and clattering of the coupling. With relief, I stepped safely in the next car.

I was really impressed when we entered the dining car. It looked like one of the finest restaurants in the world. We were shown to our own table with a starched, snow-white tablecloth and matching napkins. Sitting in the center of the table were silver servers for cream and sugar, an elegant silver vase containing fresh, colorful flowers, and a silver dish of delicious strawberry jam with a fine, silver serving spoon. The smiling Black stewards who waited on the tables wore white pants, white jackets, and white shirts with black bow ties. How did they stay clean? Imagine trying to eat spaghetti with tomato sauce dressed like that. Their shoes were well shined too, but I expected them to be. Just like my brothers and I, lots of Blacks shined shoes on the streets of Chicago.

Jerry ordered food for both of us. My breakfast was two fried eggs, sausage, fried potatoes, toast, applesauce, and a large glass of milk. Jerry had the same, but coffee instead of milk. I spread lots of strawberry jam on my toast.

"What kind of ship were you on?" I asked when I finally took a break from shoveling down the delicious food.

"A destroyer," Jerry said. "The USS Cone. DD866."

He said the ship's name like he was talking about a pretty girl.

I didn't know much about Navy ships, but the destroyer sounded impressive. I loved war films with the fearless sailors manning blazing anti-aircraft guns. Those heroes blasted the Jap Kamikazes out of the sky. The enemy planes and their pilots were a ball of flames when they crashed in the ocean.

"I'm a signalman," Jerry said. He raised his arms and put them in awkward positions. "This means all clear ahead. It's called semaphore."

I tried to copy Jerry's arm motions, but got tangled up. He smiled and again showed me the right way. I did better the second time and felt good about myself.

"Are you going back to your ship?" I asked.

"No, I'm not, Mickey. I've been assigned to recruiting duty in Cheyenne, Wyoming."

"What's recruiting?"

"I'll help other young men decide if the Navy is the right place for them."

Recruiting sounded like an important job, but not nearly as exciting as being on a fast moving, gun-firing warship.

CHAPTER FOUR

After we finished our delicious breakfast, Jerry and I worked our way back to our seats. I had a full stomach and a friend. I walked steadier with the motion of the train this time. I plopped back in my seat. I gave Jerry a smile as he sat down across from me. I felt more confident about the future of my crazy life.

"What's your family like, Jerry?" I asked.

He looked off in the distance, like he struggled to remember.

"My mother is so wonderful," he said. "I'd do anything for her."

He looked really happy as he thought about his mother.

I tried to remember how wonderful my mother was. I wanted to brag about her, but no words came to me. All I remembered was she gave me to the monster Naomi. A kid doesn't tell anyone their own mother didn't want them anymore. A kid doesn't brag that their own mother gave them to a horrible stranger and they were a helpless slave for four brutal years.

Jerry turned back to me with a more serious expression on his face.

"My Dad was really strict with my brother and me. He was easier on my sister."

"Was he mean?" I asked. "Did he hit you a lot?"

"Oh, no, it wasn't that. He didn't believe in hitting. He laid down strict rules about life, though. He didn't tolerate lying or stealing. Things like that."

Jerry paused. I watched him closely. I wondered about having a father who wasn't a liar and thief. I wondered about having a father who didn't make jokes about me looking like the milkman. I couldn't imagine a father who didn't tease me all the time and make me dream terrible nightmares. I couldn't believe fathers existed who didn't hit their children. I couldn't believe there were fathers who didn't abandon their families and leave them poor and desperate.

I sure didn't want Jerry to know how big a thief I'd been. After reading the Bible and really paying attention to the Ten Commandments, I understood how wrong it was to steal. Being forced to steal by Naomi certainly took the fun out of it.

I told plenty of lies during my life. Sometimes it was really tough not to lie. If God knew you wanted to be honest, he might forgive some mistakes. Being alone, without my brothers, I was more afraid to sin. Being alone with my sins and feeling guilty about so much of what I did in my life was awful. Hell sounded like the worst place of all and I didn't want to spend forever in that flaming pit in the center of the earth.

"My dad and I get along great now," Jerry said. "I really do love him, but I was glad to finish high school and join the Navy. The Navy has been good to me. What about you, Mickey?"

"What about me?"

Jerry smiled. "Sure. Why are you on this train trip?"

I glanced out my window. The sun was up in the sky and

15

warming the countryside. We passed a herd of cows. Mothers and babies were grazing peacefully. Some of the babies nuzzled up to the mothers and nursed. Under the glowing sun and puffy white clouds, what I saw looked like a happy scene from a school reading book. Then, I remembered the awful tour of the Chicago stockyards and the terrible slaughterhouse killing floor. I saw the swing of the sledgehammer and watched stunned cows tumble onto blood-drenched concrete floors. I didn't want to see those animal's horrible deaths as the real truth of the world.

"Oh. Uh. I'm going back to live with my mother again."

"Were you living with your Dad?"

"No. I just lived with some people." I didn't want to talk about Naomi. The memory of her and my time with her was too shameful. I wanted to keep her locked away deep inside of me. I wouldn't ever tell anyone about those terrible times.

"How long has it been since you've seen your mother, Mickey?" Jerry asked.

"Uh..." I paused. I needed to think. "It's been four years."

"Wow. That's a long time, Mickey. You must be really excited about seeing her again."

I looked down so Jerry couldn't see my face. I struggled for an answer. I didn't know how to express the way I felt.

"I'll bet your mother is excited about seeing you again," Jerry prompted.

I locked my hands together and held them between my legs. I dug my fingernails in my palms until I felt pain. My whole world turned blurry.

"Yeah," I replied without looking at Jerry. Coming through the blur, Emil appeared before me. He said those awful words again. "Your mother said she doesn't want you to come back to her. She said she doesn't have room for you."

I struggled to recall Mom's face. I couldn't imagine her saying those horrible words. Still, I really didn't know how she felt about me. She always told me she didn't have a choice when she left me with strangers. She swore she only did what she was forced to do. My stomach twisted in a knot. How would I ever know the truth?

I controlled my sadness. I turned back to Jerry with a forced smile. He looked at me for a few seconds.

"Have you been to Ogden, Utah, before, Mickey?"

"No, I never have. Mostly, I've lived in Chicago. I was born in Chicago. My mother has a new husband in Utah. I haven't met him yet. I hope he's not mean."

"I'm sure he'll be nice," Jerry said.

"Yeah," I said hopefully. "Maybe he'll be nice."

A passenger struggled to keep his balance as he walked down the train aisle holding onto seat backs. With difficulty, he slid open the doors to the vestibule and let in a rush of loud train noise. The doors slammed shut behind him and Jerry and I could hear each other again.

"Hey, Jerry," I said. "You want to see my comic books."

"Yes I would, Mickey."

I took my comic books out of the paper bag I carried all of my stuff in. I spread them out in a fan shape and counted them.

"Seven is all I have right now," I said. "I really like war comics."

My favorite comic books were the Korean War titles. The badly outnumbered G.I.'s slogged through mud and rain in always cold, dismal Korea. They blasted away at the charging Commie Gooks. With the sling wrapped around his massive forearm, a grim, unshaven, muscular American soldier fired a Browning automatic rifle. He sprayed deadly bursts from his huge gun and killed dozens of the crazy-eyed enemy. His eyes were hard, determined and fearless. I imagined being him. I wanted to be a real GI, but to be big, muscular, and fearless seemed impossible for puny me. If I magically became a super-hero, I could defeat the enemy hordes. It happened in the comic books and movies.

"I like the war comics too," Jerry said.

"Yeah," I agreed. "They're the best."

"Do you have any brothers or sisters, Mickey?" Jerry asked.

I thought for a moment. "I have four brothers."

"That sounds great, Mickey. How old are they?"

I looked down. I scratched my knee, which protruded from a sizable hole in my pant leg. "I have two older brothers and two younger brothers."

"Are they with your mother?"

I looked back up at Jerry.

"Ben is with her now. He's older than me. I haven't seen or talked to any of my brothers for four years, except for my younger brother, Steve. I saw him a month ago. We visited him for a half-hour. He's ten-years-old. He lives just outside of Chicago. He lives in a nice house and he wears nice clothes."

I looked down again. It wasn't right Steve and I couldn't be together. I stuck my right index finger in one of the holes in my pant leg. I pushed hard and dug my fingernail in my leg until I felt pain.

"Steve was adopted," I said. To say that word really hurt. Steve had a different last name than me. Of course, my last name was "Johnson" for four years. I still didn't understand why Naomi changed my name to hers when she hated me so much.

"Steve was adopted by a rich woman." Voicing that out loud made me feel better. At least someone rich wanted Steve.

"The rich woman almost adopted me and my older brother, Ben," I said. "She just didn't have room for all three of us."

"Really?" Jerry said. He looked confused and concerned.

"Honest! After that, I lived with a nice, older couple for close to a year. They wanted to adopt me, but it didn't work out. My Mom really wanted me to come back home with her. And, I wanted to be back with my two older brothers."

"Hey, can I read a couple of your comic books, Mickey?" Jerry asked. I think he realized talking about my past was painful for me.

"Sure," I handed him my whole collection, so he could choose.

He decided to read all of them. He quickly got absorbed in their adventures.

I shifted around in my seat to look out my window. I needed to forget the past. I didn't want to think about the reunion with my mother and what it'd be like when we first saw each other again. Getting back together with Mom and knowing how much I didn't trust her anymore made me want to throw up. How the hell was I supposed to act towards her? How would she act towards me? I didn't want Mom to know I never wanted her to hug me again. I didn't want her to know how much she hurt me. I didn't want to cry in front of her. I didn't want to cry in front of anyone, ever again.

I needed to forget all the depressing stuff. I wanted to enjoy the train trip. This was my first view of the real western United States. The country flowing past my window was very different from the Wild West I'd seen in the Saturday matinee movies starring Gene Autry, Hopalong Cassidy, and Bob Steele. In the cowboy films, the gangs of outlaws and the posses chasing them rode down wide dirt trails with trees all around, and shot at each other from behind large piles of huge boulders. This country I crossed was mostly flat and the edge of the earth was many miles distant. The western movies in the theatres were in black and white. The colors I saw now were as varied as what I saw when I looked through a round, cardboard kaleidoscope.

The flatness of the green Nebraska farmland had gradually changed to a sea of red grass carpeting an endless procession of bigger and bigger hills. As we entered Wyoming, the red prairie grass gave way to purplish sagebrush and the Rocky Mountains dominated the landscape. The low-lying scrubland looked bone-dry. The distant, white-snow topped mountains looked to be a land of towering green trees, crystal-clear lakes, and rushing rivers. This west was huge, with limitless, bright blue to stark white sky.

"Cheyenne, Wyoming is the next stop in ten minutes," the conductor called out as he walked through our car. "Cheyenne is the next stop."

"We're getting close to where I get off," Jerry said. "I've been thinking, Mickey. I'd like to make a deal with you. I really like fried chicken. I'll pay you five dollars for your package of fried chicken."

"Really," I stared at Jerry. "Wow. That's a lot of money, Jerry."

"I think it's a fair price."

"Well sure," I said. "If you really want the chicken, Jerry, I'll sell it to you."

Jerry opened his wallet. He counted out five one-dollar bills and handed them to me. I handed him my greasy package of fried chicken. I stuffed the money in my pants pocket. I couldn't believe my good fortune.

The train slowed as we approached Cheyenne, Wyoming. The vast and pure wilderness I admired so much changed to another clutter of buildings and a small city crowded with people. This was supposed to be the real west, the land of cowboys, but I wasn't impressed. It sure didn't look like it would be a happy place for a sailor like Jerry. Cheyenne was too distant from the ocean and Navy ships.

Cheyenne's downtown buildings sort of looked western. Some of the people on the streets were dressed like westerners in a cowboy movie. A few men wore fancy cowboy boots, tight blue jeans, belts with large buckles, elaborately patterned and colored western shirts, and real ten-gallon hats. A couple of women wore gaudy, swirly skirts, frilly blouses and five-gallon hats. I was sure there were lots of shiny pearl buttons on the men and the women's shirts and blouses.

I didn't see any low-slung holsters holding deadly six-guns. I didn't see any fancy chaps or shiny spurs. No saddled horses were tied to rails ready for a quick getaway. Some of the young men did look like they could be bronco busters or bull riders. I didn't see anyone dressed in my favorite color for a cowboy outfit; all black from head to toe like Bob Steele from the western movies always wore.

The train jerked to a stop. Steam whooshed. Metal groaned.

"Good luck to you, Mickey," Jerry said as he stood up to leave.

"Good luck to you, Jerry."

I fought the goddamn misty feeling forcing its way in my eyes. I couldn't let Jerry see me being a crybaby. He shook my hand like I was a grown-up friend of his. He turned and walked down the aisle. I watched his retreating back.

With his white sailor's hat perched atop his head and carrying his sea bag over his shoulder, Jerry stepped down onto the station platform. I waved to him through the window. He waved back and gave me a close-friend kind of smile. Despite being a big fan of soldiers, I now thought sailors wore the best-looking uniforms. Jerry disappeared as the train pulled out of Cheyenne.

It really hurt to lose a friend like Jerry. I was surprised someone like him was so friendly to a ragged kid like me. I hope he enjoys the fried chicken. I was sure he overpaid me and I felt a bit guilty.

CHAPTER FIVE

The jerky movement of the train smoothed out as we picked up speed and left Cheyenne behind us.

We climbed higher in pine tree covered mountains. Soon, we rolled into a more western looking town. Laramie was home to the University of Wyoming, the sign read. Nobody in my family went to a university. I wasn't sure if any member of my family graduated from high school. I was told without a high school degree, I was doomed. Graduating from high school was my number one goal in life and then I'd move on to a better future. An eight minute stop in Laramie didn't produce any interesting new passengers in my car.

A couple of hours later, we arrived in Rawlins, home to the State Penitentiary. Thoughts of murderers and robbers locked behind the high, barbwire-topped concrete walls worried me. I looked in both directions from my window to check the new passengers who boarded the train. I wanted to make sure no murderous, prison escapees were among them.

"Lunch will be served in the dining car in ten minutes," a Black porter called out as he passed through the car. With a tiny, miniature hammer, he sounded several notes on the small brass bell he held; the fancy way they announced every meal on the train.

After we'd traveled clear of Rawlins, I ventured to the dining car for lunch. I tried to walk the aisle as steady as when I went to breakfast with Jerry. I managed the doors and the space between the cars without being overwhelmed. With five dollars in my pocket, I walked in the high-class, railroad-car restaurant. The richness of the place intimidated me. I wanted to turn around and flee. The Black waiter smiled at me. To be sure he wouldn't refuse to serve me, I pulled money part way out of my pocket, so he'd see I could pay my way.

"Well, good afternoon, sir," he said, bowing slightly. "May I show you to a table?"

I knew he was having fun with me, but didn't mind. I looked forward to a great lunch.

He showed me to a small table with two chairs. He opened a menu and placed it before me.

"There you are, sir."

Man, he was having fun with me. He wasn't being mean though. I recognized meanness in people right away. I stopped reading the menu as soon as I found the cheeseburger.

I wished the chair across from me wasn't empty. It would be perfect if Jerry sat there. Despite the money I carried, my poor slum boy clothes made me feel totally out of place in this fancy dining car. I should be eating hot dogs from a cart on the dirty streets of Chicago. Some of the passengers who entered the dining car stared at me. Finally, a handsome young couple gave me a friendly smile. At least there was someone who didn't see me as a dirty, thieving, street boy. I felt more at ease.

The young couple were the kind of people I'd like to be adopted by.

I enjoyed a delicious lunch. My stomach full from a cheeseburger, fries, and apple pie with ice cream, I worked my way back to my seat. Except for being alone again, I felt good. Jerry shook my hand and wished me good luck when he left the train in Cheyenne. I'd remember him and his kindness for a long time.

I sat back in my seat and the steady clacking rhythm of the train wheels began lulling me to sleep. I needed to stay awake, though. I sat up straight and looked out my window. I didn't want to miss any of these wonderful, wild-west sights.

As the train rolled deeper in Wyoming, I spotted a herd of grazing antelope. They were small, just a bit larger than a goat. Their appearance really surprised me. I thought they'd be much bigger; closer to the size of a buffalo. Their coloring was an exotic blend of brown and white stripes and patches. As we rattled past them, their short-horned heads popped up. They appeared frightened, launched into movement and ran faster than any animal I'd ever seen. The last I saw of them was their brilliant-white rumps and small clouds of dust left by their little feet. If I'd imagined an animal like them, I'd have pictured Africa as their home.

The back-and-forth sideway train movements caused nausea to creep up on me again. I hated the ready-to-puke feeling. I gave up on sightseeing, stretched out on my seat and closed my eyes. This time, no demons attacked me. I dozed off and Wyoming rolled away under the train wheels.

. . .

A hand on my shoulder woke me. The friendly conductor towered over me. "We crossed the state line into Utah, son. You'll be home soon."

"Thank you, sir." Oh well. He didn't understand. Nobody understood. I didn't have a home.

The train slowed as we entered steep-walled canyons. I switched to a seat on the other side of the car to see we were at the edge of a scary, steep drop-off. A rushing river far below us shimmered with bright green, blue, and white colors.

The train roared into a tunnel. My car became dark except for the dim lights along the floor of the center aisle. Through the windows, I watched green, orange, and red signal lights flash by and blend in a single color. It was like a ride through the tunnel of horrors in an amusement park, except on this train, no ghosts popped up from the shadows to frighten me.

We burst back in bright daylight. We were still on the scary edge of a precipice. I moved back to my own seat. I pushed my face against the window so I could see the top of the canyon wall rising menacingly to the sky on that side of the tracks. Twisting my head back and forth, I looked ahead and to the rear. The rapidly passing multicolored-stone wall turned to a dizzying blur.

My neck hurt, so I sat back and rested. I closed my eyes. This time, demons swirled in the blackness. Naomi was the cruelest of all. I hoped she was burning in the red-hot fires of hell. I hoped every day of the week the devil stabbed her with his blazing-hot pitchfork.

I took the photograph Virginia sent with my train ticket out of my paper bag. I studied the black and white picture of her and my new stepsister. A beautiful forest was close behind them. Peggy's head rested against Virginia's chest. Peggy's arms were wrapped around Virginia's waist. Virginia's arms held Peggy tight to her. They both smiled beautifully and looked completely happy. Even though I didn't want anyone to hold me like they held each other, I felt a terrible surge of jealousy.

Virginia wore a matching black jacket and skirt with a white blouse. Peggy wore a cream-colored dress that came just below her knees. White rolled-down socks revealed her lovely legs. Their clothes fit them perfectly. They were both pretty. They both looked absolutely normal. The photograph showed a perfect mother and daughter that loved being together.

I couldn't imagine growing up with a real sister. The last time I lived with my mother, it was my two older brothers and me getting in trouble. When Virginia locked Tommy, Ben and me in our room while she went to work, we were confined together for hours with metal buckets for a toilet. We eventually climbed out through our window to the fire escape and were free from our stinking, sweltering prison. The three of us roamed across rooftops, ran down strange, dark stairways, and shouted shit, fuck, and goddamn to celebrate our freedom.

There wasn't any place for a girl in our gang wandering the dangerous streets of Chicago. We pissed in alleys, shit in bushes in the parks along the lakefront, got in fistfights, rolled drunks, conned money from men who were looking for lonely young boys to have sex with, stole from everyone, and constantly ran from the coppers.

Our everyday shenanigans weren't any kind of life for a girl like Peggy in the photograph. I was sure a sister would've been much different than we'd been. She would've always been clean, well dressed, and well behaved. I was sure Virginia wouldn't have given a daughter away to strangers to be a slave like she'd done with me.

Why was I, a slum boy and giveaway child, returning to live with my mother? I knew she didn't want me to come out to this Utah place and mess up her new family. I'd embarrass her. I could see from the photograph that she liked her new daughter a lot. In the photograph, Peggy was the prettiest girl I ever saw. She certainly wouldn't want anything to do with someone like me.

I tried to remember the look of my mother from when I was young, lived with her, and she loved me. I tried to remember the sound, smell, and feel of her. Hell. That was baby stuff. All that crap was little sissy-boy foolishness. Mother love was a huge lie. I wouldn't ever fall in that trap again. I was on my own in life and needed to look out for myself. Nobody else cared what happened to me.

My mother was so easy to love when I was young. Even after she lied to me and gave me away, I always weakened and couldn't stay mad at her. I always wanted to love her and wanted her to love me. It should be easy for me to hate her. Why the hell couldn't I hate her all the time? Why was she always the winner?

I put the photograph back in my paper bag. I pressed my face against the cold glass of the train window. I was trapped. I had to go back to her. I didn't have anywhere else to go. I didn't have anyone else to turn to for help. I wanted to disappear through the thick glass and stay behind in the wilderness. I wanted to live in a world without people and their cruelty. I wanted to live in a world where nobody slapped my face. I wanted to live in a world where nobody kicked me. I'd kill the next person that did.

Jesus Christ. I was trapped on this goddamn train because of my cowardly fear of all the bullies in the world. I was afraid to live on my own. I was a weakling.

I had to get stronger.

I had to get meaner.

CHAPTER SIX

The conductor gave me a smile as he steadied himself in the train aisle.

"Ogden, Utah is the next stop, son."

"Thank you, sir."

It appeared he expected me to be excited and happy about arriving in Ogden, Utah. Instead, his words felt like a slap to my face.

"Ogden, Utah," he called out through the car as he continued down the aisle. "Population, 65,000." He slid open the vestibule door and disappeared in the blast of noise.

My long journey was over. The train screeched and rattled as we rolled into the station. At first, I thought those steel-on-steel screeches were screams coming from my parched throat. But, I hadn't screamed out in fear. I was frozen in silence by my dread of the reunion about to happen.

Emil's words were seared in my brain. "Your mother said she didn't want you to come back to her. Your mother said she didn't have room for you."

For me to believe Mom really spoke those horrible words

was too painful. It was better to think Emil was a liar and live with that as the truth. It was too late for me to make an escape from her and her new family.

It seemed like forever since I'd seen my mother. Four years of silence. Damn her to hell. Why didn't she communicate with me? Did she hate me so much?

I looked out my window. There weren't many people on the platform. Station workers pushed baggage carts in position. When we finally came to a full stop, they opened the baggage compartment doors along the bottom of the train. Workers lowered steps under the doors for disembarking. It was time for me to leave the safety of my passenger car.

What if my mother didn't show up to take me back? What if she moved and I wouldn't ever find her? What if she took one look at me, didn't like what she saw, and decided to give me away again?

I saw a slender, blond woman anxiously searching the train windows. She reminded me of my mother. She wore a matching, dark-blue jacket and skirt and high heel shoes.

The blond woman looked at me.

She stared at me.

Her stare changed to a big smile.

She waved to me.

I recognized her. It was my mother. She changed the color of her hair from black to blond. She was more Hollywood glamorous than I remembered.

With tremors coursing through my legs I stood.

I wobbled.

I lurched along the center aisle of the train.

I dragged my feet forward.

I took the last steps on my way to stand under the hangman's noose.

Shaking with fear, I slid open the doors and entered the vestibule. I turned right.

Terribly weak, I clumsily descended four metal steps.

She strode towards me as I stepped down to the platform. She encircled me with a bone-crushing hug. I couldn't stop her.

"I'm so happy to see you," she said close to my ear. Her lips touched my cheek. She held me tight to her body. She enveloped me in her warm perfume smell. Terrified by her show of affection, I couldn't make my body respond. I longed for her embrace and protection during my first heart-crushing months as a slave to Naomi. My hopeful dream she'd rush back to rescue me from the monster turned to a four-year nightmare. I wouldn't fall in that trap again. My arms hung lifeless against my sides. My mouth refused to smile. When she finally released me, I didn't fall over as I feared I might. I took a deep breath. I told myself not to be afraid of my mother. Never again, would I let her, or anyone else, give me away in slavery.

I didn't have a coat and I shivered from a gust of cold air.

"You're so thin," she said. I glanced up at her. It looked like she held back tears. She flashed another smile down at me. It was like she thought a smile would make everything better. My mother promised she'd come back as soon as she could and rescue me from the monster, Naomi. But, she never showed up. She was a goddamn liar. I hated her self-serving smile. I hated her.

"Mickey," she nodded towards the man who stood just behind her. "This is your new stepfather, Al Davey."

Al Davey wore workman's clothes of neatly pressed, matching dark-green shirt and pants. He stood about six-foot-one, with thinning black hair and pockmarked, olive complexion. He smiled down at me and offered a handshake. His hairy hand was massive, but he didn't try to crush my small hand. The thick black hair curling over the top of his white tee shirt reminded me of burly immigrant workers in Chicago. Kindness radiated from him. My fear of another cruel stepfather didn't disappear completely, but it lessened.

"And this is your new sister, Peggy."

My new sister, Peggy, nodded at me. She gave me a forced smile.

"Hi," She said quietly. Peggy appeared embarrassed by my skinny, raggedy look. She acted discomforted by having to acknowledge me as someone connected to her.

I knew I was a sad excuse for a human being and I expected negative responses from most normal people.

My voice deserted me. Like a rabbit caught in a trapper's snare, I stood helpless as these three strangers towered over and studied me. I had no place to hide. I looked down at my feet.

"Peggy's thirteen," Virginia said, "You and she are only a year apart in age."

Peggy, though only a year older than me, was much taller than I was. She was also pretty. With thick, light-brown, shoulder length hair, large brown eyes and clear fair skin, I thought she was the most perfect girl I'd ever been this close to. She wore a silky, rose-colored dress that fell just below her knees. What was exposed of her legs made me feel light-headed.

Virginia put her arm across Peggy's shoulders. Peggy snuggled up to Virginia, wrapped her arms around Virginia's waist, and rested her head against my mother's chest. They stood in front of me just like they'd posed in the photograph I carried in my paper bag.

Did Peggy notice my lack of response when Virginia hugged me? I thought her expression showed relief. She acted just like my brothers, years ago, when they owned all of our mother's attention for themselves, and thought she loved them more than she loved me. The return of the abandoned son didn't pose a threat to Peggy's hold on my mother's love and affection.

"Where's your suitcase, Mickey?" Virginia asked.

"I don't have one. All my stuff is in my paper bag."

"You have more clothes in there?"

"I have a pair of underwear and a pair of socks."

"We need to get you some clothes," she said with concern. She ran her hand through my hair. I knew she wouldn't hit me, but I flinched. My "expecting-to-be-hit" fear overwhelmed me when anyone thrust their hands toward my face.

I followed the three strangers through the train station and out to a parking lot. I obeyed their instructions to climb in their dark-green, four-door sedan.

CHAPTER SEVEN

I sat in the back seat of the car with my new stepsister Peggy. I held my paper bag containing all my worldly possessions on my lap. She sat as close to her door as possible and as far away from me as she could. I snuck sideway glances at her and was glad she didn't look back at me.

As we drove, the darkness of night overtook us and streetlights began to glow along the avenues of Ogden, Utah.

"We'll make a quick stop at the Salvation Army," Virginia said, as she turned and smiled back at me from the front seat. "Maybe we can find some nice clothes for you, Mickey."

I hadn't ever heard of the Salvation Army. It sounded like a strange place to buy new clothes. Maybe, I'd end up dressed like a soldier in the war movies. That was fine with me.

"Thanks," I said. I didn't know how to address my mother. I didn't want to call her Mom. I hated that word. I decided for now, I wouldn't call her by any name or title. I just needed to make some kind of noise to get her attention. I'd figure out a way.

"Emil said Ben was living with you."

"Ben's visiting your father in California."

Damn. Ben always said he'd find our father. I didn't want to see my cruel bastard of a father ever again. It was seven years since he'd walked out on our family and he'd taken Baby John with him to California. I was glad to see the mean bully disappear. I could tell by Virginia's tone she didn't really want to talk about my brothers. I was afraid to press any subject and irritate her and give her a reason to get rid of me again.

We drove several blocks, made a couple of turns, crept down a narrow alley, and parked behind a two-story brick building.

We entered the building through the back door. We walked through a large, restaurant-type kitchen. It was warm inside and filled with the noise of clanging pans and smells of cooking food.

"This is my son, Mickey," Virginia introduced me to several people who worked in the kitchen. A stout, gray-haired woman, who wore a loose-fitting, flowery housedress and a white apron, smiled at me. She was stirring the contents of a large metal pot that bubbled and gave off clouds of steam and boiling vegetable odors.

Next we entered a room crowded with long, wooden tables and benches. A fat, middle-aged man with a red, bulbous nose nodded at me as he continued to remove the wrappers from blocks of yellow butter. A more aged man, whose deeply-wrinkled hands trembled, gave me a toothless grin as he took loaves of clear-cellophane wrapped, white-bread out of a cardboard box and stacked them on a table.

More plainly-dressed, saggy-shaped people laid out silverware and napkins on the tables in the dining room. Virginia placed her hand on my shoulder and spoke out to them, "This is my son, Mickey." Some stopped momentarily for nods of recognition as we walked through. I hated being pointed out to people and made the center of attention. At least the people working here didn't look much better than I did.

A double wide door opened to the thrift store. It was a large space with multiple aisles of appliances, furniture, dishes, children's toys, and books. Clothing of every sort hung from racks and lay piled in bins. The array of garments didn't look new, nor completely worn out. Virginia picked out a couple of colorful, striped tee shirts, a pair of denim trousers, a leather belt, and a dark-blue, wool pea coat for me.

"These should fit you, Mickey," she said optimistically. She held each garment of my new wardrobe against my skinny body. They looked too big to me, but I'd be glad to never again wear the raggedy, oversized, old-man clothes Naomi forced me to wear everywhere when I was her slave. I stumbled about in that goddamn clown outfit for four, horrifying years.

Virginia carefully counted out money and paid for my slightly-used clothes. We said our goodbyes and drove to my new family's home. We turned in the driveway alongside their house. From the outside, it didn't look bad.

The small, white painted, wood house Virginia and her new husband, Al Davey, rented, stood two stories high, with a living room, dining area and kitchen downstairs and two bedrooms and a single bathroom upstairs.

After tensing my way through another of Virginia's attempts at a motherly hug and kiss, I crawled in my sleeping place on a narrow cot in the upstairs hallway. I heard Al Davey and my mother move about in their room. Far more intriguing, I listened closely and heard my new stepsister Peggy's movements in her room as she prepared for bed.

I laid in the darkness on the uncomfortable hallway cot. I thought. I wondered. I knew I wouldn't have a room of my own. I was still an unwanted interloper. But, life had to be better here. The horror of Naomi, the woman my mother callously gave me to, was behind me. I needed to forget about my endless hours of laboring as her house slave. The monster had screamed curses at me, called me stupid, slapped my face, punched me with her big fists, and beat me with her broomstick. While I cowered on the floor, she kicked me like I was a stray dog. I cringed before her like the frightened curs I saw slinking through Chicago's filthy alleys. I wanted to kill Naomi for the terrible way she treated me, but luckily, the monster died before I killed her. If she hadn't died, and I killed her with my own hands, I would've been a convicted murderer. The coppers would've strapped me in the electric chair. They would've pulled a black hood down over my head. I would've screamed for mercy, but the coppers would've laughed as they pulled down a big switch and fried me to a crisp.

I sobbed without understanding why.

Finally, a deep sleep without nightmares rescued me.

CHAPTER EIGHT

The next morning, a deep-blue sky greeted me as I stepped down to the concrete sidewalk from the front porch of my mother's house. I took in my sunny, but chilly, new world. I looked to my left up the avenue. A couple of miles in that direction, houses ended and desolate, sagebrush-covered foothills rose. Those foothills were dwarfed as they merged with the snow-topped Wasatch Mountains towering forty-five-hundred feet above Ogden, Utah. The massive range of peaks was both startling, and awe-inspiring.

To my right, the city of Ogden, absent of hundreds of tall buildings like those that dominated Chicago, descended and disappeared in a white, hazy plain, the Great Salt Lake Desert. It wasn't the colorful, cactus and lizard filled kind of desert I always wanted to explore and maybe live in. It was a flat, life-less plain consisting mostly of salt.

I took a deep breath. The crisp mountain air shocked my city-raised lungs. I stood in a world far different from the Chicago I'd grown up in. No canyons were formed by brick and stone buildings reaching for the clouds. No thousand smoke-

stacks belched their black and gray, sky-fouling plumes. No
streetcars or elevated trains screeched and groaned along steel
tracks. No non-stop honking of truck and car horns and
screams of factory whistles tortured my ears. No loud, brassy
symphony of shouting and cursing voices in dialects gathered
from every part of the world made me flinch.

I listened to the early morning song of birds and the chatter
of squirrels. A slight breeze rustled through the shade trees
lining both sides of the avenue. A couple of cars and a small
delivery truck drove unhurried along the street. Out in front of
a house down the block, the happy voice of a child greeting the
new day pierced the calm.

But not everything was changed for me. I faced a new
school. In school, I faced new children. Children were unpre-
dictable and many times terribly cruel. Fear settled in my gut. I
was sure danger lurked around every corner of my new world.

"Mickey," Virginia called from inside the house. "Come in
and eat breakfast."

As I walked back inside my new home to face my mother,
Virginia, and my new life with her, apprehension surged
through my body. But, I didn't want fear to show on my face. I
didn't want her, my new family, or anyone else to see how
scared I was. I was trapped here and didn't have any other
option. I didn't trust anyone. I didn't think I'd ever completely
trust any human the rest of my life.

I entered the small kitchen crowded with white appliances,
and a table and four matching chairs made out of shiny chrome
and green plastic. Virginia greeted me with a warm smile. I
avoided another unnerving motherly-hug by dodging away
from her. I sat on the chair directly across from my new stepsister, Peggy. Her prettiness hadn't faded one bit overnight. She
wore a short-sleeved blue dress with a below-the-knee skirt
flaring out around her lovely legs. She'd already eaten half of

one egg and a slice of toast. She gave me a brief, forced smile and continued her dainty consumption of her tiny amount of food.

Virginia fried two eggs for me. She tenderly served them with smiles and two slices of buttered toast. She placed her hand on my shoulder and I flinched. Damn. I still didn't have any control over my reactions. I hated to be touched by her or anyone. Less than a day back with her and I already had my fill of her shows of motherly warmth. I knew despite her attempts at affection, she could easily change and abandon me at any moment. Any feelings I ever felt for her were shriveled up in a foul lump lying dead inside of me. That lump of deadness caused my gut to tighten and ache whenever I interacted with her. I was hungry though, so I forced away my bad feelings. I ate breakfast sitting directly across from my fascinating new stepsister, Peggy. She couldn't avoid me. After four years of being bullied and ostracized by most people and especially by kids my age, I couldn't believe my great fortune in having this wonderful girl living in the same house as worthless me.

Peggy mostly tried to pretend I wasn't there. That was fine with me. If she didn't look at me, I could stare at her. When she did look at me directly, my courage immediately crumbled and I looked away. I realized I had to spy on her. I stared at a crumb of toast in the corner of her mouth. She saw me. She wiped away the crumb. She gave me a look of intense irritation and abruptly stood. She rushed off and ran up the stairs to the second floor. A door slammed shut. I bet she was in the bathroom brushing her pretty, white teeth. I hadn't owned a toothbrush since I lived with George and Rose, five years ago. Maybe, I'll get one now.

CHAPTER NINE

From my Mother's house, it was only four blocks to the new school I'd attend. I wore my newly acquired, second-hand Salvation Army clothes. My hands disappeared in the too-long sleeves of my second hand, dark-blue pea coat.

"Don't worry, Mickey." Virginia assured me. "You'll fatten up and lengthen out. Then, the clothes will fit you perfectly."

I didn't believe any clothes would ever fit my wretched body anywhere close to perfect.

"Living in Ogden is going to be quite different from living in Chicago," she said as we walked to the school. "It's much safer here and a lot cleaner."

"Yeah," I replied. "It sure looks different." I was in the Wild West, but so far, not much resembled the movie version of the west I'd looked forward to.

Virginia didn't have any idea how horrible the last four years were for me in Chicago, living as Naomi's slave and prisoner. I sensed she wouldn't ever want to know how I suffered. My mother didn't like to talk about bad things in life, and she especially didn't like to talk about bad things she did to her sons.

Did my mother care at all about what occurred while I was out of sight and far from her protection? I didn't know. She acted like everything was hunky-dory. I needed to forget about the Naomi horrors. My life with the monster was too wretched and shameful to think or talk about.

Kids converged on my new school from all directions. They arrived on foot, in school buses and in cars driven by parents. Most of the children appeared to be happy as they gathered in groups and interacted playfully. I didn't see nearly as much fear on their young faces as I'd seen at Ryerson School in Chicago.

Being too different from the rest of the world is really frightening. If you have a big scar or big birthmark on your face, you are painfully different from everyone else. If you have big ears sticking out like Dumbo the cartoon elephant, too big or too small of a nose, or you are too fat or too skinny, or too short or too tall, you would be in for a hard time as a kid. The bullies would descend upon you like a swarm of gnats.

Many of the children approached the school with a gliding nimbleness that shouted confidence. I tried to walk the way a kid was supposed to walk when his shoes fit. My legs still wanted to work like they did at Naomi's when I staggered about like a skid row drunk. Then, I struggled to maintain my balance in the oversized clodhoppers the monster forced me to wear. The memory of those times made me want to puke.

Even though the clothes my mother bought for me at the Salvation Army store were too big, I didn't look like the freak Naomi turned me into by forcing me to wear raggedy, over-sized, old-man clothes.

. . .

Virginia and I walked past groups of students that thankfully ignored us. We found our way and entered an office to register me at my new place of learning. Lewis Junior High school was a three-story, reddish-brown brick building. Shade trees, green lawns, and wide walkways separated the education fortress from the streets on all four sides.

A display of award-winning student artwork hung on the walls outside the office. I liked one of the crude drawings in particular. It showed a group of men with devilish looking faces firing rifles at two fallen victims. Bullets entered bodies. Blood spurted. The shot men held their hands up to the shooters and the heavens as they pleaded for mercy. The words under the amateurish artwork said: *On June 27, 1844 the Prophet Joseph Smith and his brother Hyrum were brutally assassinated by enemies of the Church in the county jail at Carthage, Illinois.*

At first, I read the words wrong. I read Chicago in place of Carthage and was relieved when I reread it correctly. I never heard of Carthage and didn't want to be from such a place. My hometown, Chicago, was a famous city and had plenty of its own shootings, but those were mostly gangsters killing other gangsters.

A middle-aged woman wearing a brown blazer, matching straight skirt, and white blouse greeted us. Her brown hair was in a wavy perm. She wore glasses and her expression was super serious.

"How can I help you?"

"We want to register my son in school."

"Do you have the records from his previous school?"

"No, I don't," Virginia said. "I'm sorry."

"You don't have anything at all?"

"I'm sorry, but all his records were lost."

The woman squinted at us. She adjusted her glasses. She looked across the counter and down at me.

"The school I went to was in Chicago, ma'am." I wanted to clear up any confusion quickly.

"Chicago?" she said as if she were talking about hell itself. She wrote something down. "What's your full name?"

"Mickey Johnson," I said. "Uh, I mean Mickey Shafer."

"That's your full legal name?" she questioned me with a doubting stare.

"Uh." I tried to think. I felt panic. I wasn't prepared for such a difficult test so soon.

"Robert Michael Shafer," Virginia said. "Mickey is a nickname. We've called him Mickey since he was a baby."

"Oh," she said. "Well, at his age he should go by his full legal name. No more nicknames."

Having been Mickey Johnson for four years, I found it difficult to remember my last name was Shafer, and now this woman wanted to change my first name. I didn't want to quit using "Mickey", but she acted like she was the boss of everything in the world.

"You're his mother?"

"Yes, I am. I'm remarried, so my last name is Davey now."

"Divorced and remarried. So you aren't a Mormon?"

"No we're not. We attend church services at the Salvation Army."

"I didn't know they had worship services. You don't go to church down on skid row, do you?"

"Yes we do. They have a nice chapel."

"You go to church where all those drunken Indians and other alcoholics litter the sidewalks?" She shook her head. "How awful that must be."

Virginia looked irritated, but stood her ground. She looked the woman straight in the eye. "It's not awful. It's where prayer is most needed."

"Since you're not a Mormon, Robert, you won't need to

attend the before school hour of religious study," the woman said, ignoring Virginia. "Unless you intend to convert to the Mormon religion?"

"I don't think he'll be going to the Mormon Church," Virginia said. "If he decides he wants to, he and I will talk about it."

"Oh," the woman said. Her forced smile disappeared. She looked down at me again.

"You're in the seventh grade?"

"Yes Ma'am."

"And you're twelve-years-old?"

"I'm real close to thirteen, ma'am."

"You're small for your age."

"I think he's getting ready for a growth spurt," Virginia said. "He certainly eats enough."

"We'll see how he does in the seventh grade here," the woman said doubtfully. "I'll have someone take him to his first class after you finish signing a few more forms."

"You're in your new school, Mickey," Virginia said as she prepared to leave. "I'm sure you'll like it here."

She bent down and gave me a hug and a kiss on my cheek. I really wished she wouldn't bother me with her phony affection.

"Enjoy school, honey," she said as she patted me on my shoulder. Every time she touched me I flinched. I hated how I reacted to her. I needed to learn to control my fear and reactions. I needed to adjust to my frightening new world. She finally left.

I was totally confused about all the Mormon and Salvation Army church stuff.

CHAPTER TEN

Astuck up, freckle-faced girl led me to my first class. The empty classroom was neat and clean and colorful maps hung on the walls. A large globe sat on a table and showed the entire round earth, lots of books were neatly organized on shelves, and the wooden desks were in good condition.

I took my pea coat off and held it over my arm. I wore one of the two colorful, striped tee shirts Virginia bought for me at the Salvation Army store. I stood at the front of the classroom near the teacher's desk and waited. The silence ended abruptly as the door swung open. The classroom filled with a wave of excited, well-scrubbed, and neatly dressed students. They were followed by a young and pretty teacher.

"Well," the teacher said. "We have a new student."

A few kids stared at me.

"You missed the pre-school religious study hour," a girl student declared.

"I'm not a Mormon." I forced the words out. "I'm not supposed to go."

Chatter subsided. Smiles dissipated around me.

A large, smirking, male student approached me.

"Hey, kid. I recognize the tee shirt you're wearing. It used to be mine." Tall and muscular, he grabbed the front of my shirt. "I outgrew this shirt and my mother gave it to the Salvation Army. How'd you get it?"

Goddamn. This couldn't be happening to me. But, it was. He grabbed more of my shirt in his big hand. He tugged more forcefully.

"Yes, sir. This was my shirt." He laughed loudly.

Giggles and whispers erupted. Everybody in the classroom, including the teacher, became an audience to the sneering bully's show.

I didn't say anything. I looked up at him. The contempt I saw in his expression frightened me. I looked down at my feet. There wasn't anywhere to hide. He wouldn't go away. He really enjoyed the game and the attention. He continued to pull the front of my shirt and repeated even louder, "Yeah, that shirt used to be mine. My mother gave it to the Salvation Army and here it is. The new kid is wearing my old shirt." Heat flooded my face. I was sure my skin was crimson. I hated when that happened. He finally let go of my shirt. Everyone now knew I wore secondhand clothes. The stage was set. I was slaughtered, packaged, and labeled.

The classroom door opened. ABlack girl entered. She quickly and quietly slid in her seat. The other students ignored her. She gave me a quick glance. Her eyes revealed nothing. A bit pudgy, with broad African people features and kinky, black hair, she hunched over and tried to hide. Her clothes were nice and fit her, but she was a large person for her age.

"Let's quiet down, children. Take your seats," the teacher finally interrupted the show. "You sit there." She pointed at an empty desk. There was no welcome or friendliness in her voice or eyes.

I sat down at my new desk. I wished I was invisible. But, there wasn't any possibility for me to disappear at this awful moment.

The teacher started the lesson for the day. Her words were a mumble-jumble to me. I was only concerned with how I'd survive my first day in this new hell.

The fresh-faced teacher who talked and wrote on the blackboard had freckles. I had freckles. Maybe the teacher would change her mind and like me because we both had freckles. She had light brown hair and some of the other kids in the room were almost blond. I was the blondest person in the classroom. Maybe someone would like me because of my blond hair. I was also the skinniest and most awkwardly dressed kid. The Black girl was the only Black person I'd seen in this school so far. At least I wasn't a Black person. Hopefully, these kids would hate the Black girl more than they'd hate me.

CHAPTER ELEVEN

E very Sunday morning and evening and often on Wednesday night, I attended worship services at the Salvation Army, with Virginia, Al and Peggy. This was my first formal religious experience since age seven, when I attended Catholic school and church, made my first confession, and received Holy Communion. That time as a good Catholic boy back then ended when Mom gave me to Rose and George, who didn't go to church. Although complete strangers, they were kind and generous and I liked living with them, except I missed my real family so much it hurt. Mom visited me ten months later on Christmas day and asked me to return home to her. Rose and George wanted to adopt me, and were angry I chose to leave them. It was a bad decision on my part. A year later, Mom gave me to the monster Naomi.

While confined to my room at Naomi's during that time, for hours, days, weeks, and years, I struggled to read the Bible and Pilgrims Progress which resided in the drawer of the night-stand. I was intrigued by both books. It was difficult for me to understand what the many strange words meant, but I kept reading. Those difficult books were the only reading material available to me, and the terrible boredom of isolation in that small room kept me returning to those pages.

Now that I was attending a real church again, I could have guidance to study the Bible, unlike those years at Naomi's. I could learn and memorize the complete and true story of mankind's beginning. I could learn everything there was to know about Jesus Christ, the Savior.

The Salvation Army Center, comprised of two, two-story brick buildings, stood on 25th street, three blocks from the Union Pacific Railroad Depot. This religious center was in the heart of Ogden, Utah's notorious skid row. One building housed the chapel, offices, and large dining room and kitchen downstairs. Upstairs was an apartment where the officers in charge of the center and their families lived. The thrift store took up the entire first floor of the adjoining building. Folding cots, wash-basins, toilets and showers for the temporarily homeless, and recovering alcoholic men, crowded the building's second floor.

In charge of this center were Captain and Mrs. Owens. Over six-feet-tall, athletically built and movie star handsome, Captain Owens possessed a fine base voice for singing and preaching. Mrs. Owens stood barely five-feet-tall, with long black hair, clear skin, and a lovely face. She possessed a warm smile, perfectly-tuned soprano singing voice, and excellent skill as a pianist. For me, she made the singing of hymns a highlight of the religious services. She was also blessed with a shapely body. No matter how many sins were added to my already heavy burden, I couldn't quit staring at her large breasts. Their daughter, Carol, was eleven. Their son, Bud, a miniature copy of his father, was eight. I quickly found myself in love with frail, dark-haired, doe-eyed Carol. My obsession with both her, and my new stepsister, Peggy, became a major obstruction on my road to salvation. I couldn't quit staring at and adoring both of them.

The Owens family seemed far too handsome and gifted for this lowly place of worship. The congregation was dominated by the poor and uneducated. Worshippers with oversized, pendulous breasts, protruding bellies, and feet flattened by body weight, showed zealous, but time-worn faces. Ecstatic smiles revealed bad teeth, heavily-stained yellow crooked teeth, or loose fitting, bright-white false teeth. A few caved-in, deeply-wrinkled faces revealed some people didn't have a single tooth and couldn't afford dentures.

From skid row immediately outside the front door of the chapel, disheveled drunks staggered in for the warmth. Attired in filthy, stained, ragged clothing and battered shoes, most of the lost souls spent their last dollars on cheap, sweet wine. Now, they suffered through the calls to salvation in order to obtain hot soup and buttered bread served after the services. Some simply fell asleep in the uncomfortable, wooden pews, and snored loudly through the sermons.

Al Davey's older brother, Delbert, and his wife Ida, were dedicated soldiers and the inspiration for Al and Virginia to participate in the Salvation Army. Delbert played the base drum and added his deep, base voice to the singing of the hymns. He also went forward to kneel next to, and pray with repentant sinners. Ida added her quiet voice to the singing.

I listened to many sermons. I watched people find Jesus Christ and salvation. Guilt-wracked sinners stumbled forward and knelt at the front rail beneath the pulpit. They felt the touch of Captain Owens' hand on their heads. Bodies vibrated when the ecstasy of redemption surged through them. Tears stained the floor at their feet.

"And it shall come to pass that whoever calls on the name

of the Lord shall be saved," Captain Owens read from the Bible. "The Book of Acts 2:21."

Virginia, who owned a complete, secondhand Salvation Army uniform, including the bonnet, sang the hymns with her pleasant voice. She listened to the sermons as if she believed. Occasionally she looked like she wanted to shout out "Amen", but restrained from such public outbursts. An excellent seamstress, she made alterations to her uniform and turned it to a perfect fit. An expression of kindness was natural to her face. She looked and acted like the perfect Salvation Army lassie.

I listened to the call to be saved. I felt a strong urge to walk up to the front rail and kneel. I felt the need to bow down before God. A strong desire to be close to Jesus Christ surged through me. A deep curiosity about the possibility of him knowing of my existence nagged at me. I wanted all of the wonderful words I heard to be true. I wanted to be like this Jesus. I wanted to find the peace they said Jesus found. He accepted terrible abuse, but still held his head high. I didn't want to hang my head like I did all of the time. I didn't want to hide from the bullies by crawling inside myself. I wanted to be free of my hatred for the abusers, free of my fantasies of revenge, and free of my desire to kill my enemies.

Virginia altered a used Salvation Army uniform in an attempt to make the jacket and pants fit my skinny frame. She shortened the pant legs and the sleeves of the jacket. Despite her best efforts, I filled out the uniform like a scarecrow hung in a corn field filled out its oversized, ragged, throwaway farm clothes. She couldn't alter the cap. With the oversized Salvation Army soldier cap precariously perched atop my head, and shiny, black shoes on my feet, I hoped to show my readiness for the war on sin. With a Bible in my hand, I was fully outfitted to march in the army of the Lord.

Despite being attired as a Christian soldier, one truth couldn't be altered. I was born without a singing voice. Despite my feeble efforts to improve, I was stuck with an out-of-tune wail that sent the bravest of listeners scurrying for cover.

Robotically following other people's suggestions, I took chorus in school. When I sang with any volume, forty other voices couldn't prevent my totally out-of-tune vocals from breaking through and reducing the entire class to groans and laughter. In desperation, the instructor told me to remain silent and only mouth the words.

Robotically, I signed up for instrumental band class, but my lack of musical talent and true motivation once again proved disastrous. That instructor told me when I played the sax-horn, just push the finger buttons and pretend I was blowing through the mouthpiece. The entire band sighed gratefully at my silence.

Even Jesus Christ the Lord couldn't help me overcome my musical shortcomings. I'd be better off living as a solitary wolf in the wildest of wilds, and plaintively howling at the moon.

CHAPTER TWELVE

On many evenings, the religious services I attended shifted from inside the Salvation Army Chapel, out onto the tavern-lined street directly across from the center. Into the flashing neon our small contingent of soldiers marched, our brassy music rolling in the night. I wore my ill-fitted Salvation Army soldier uniform and struggled to balance the baritone horn on my shoulder. Traffic stopped momentarily, as we Salvationists crossed the busy street to claim our station at the saloon-side curb. We lined up neatly in the gutter and faced a depressing parade of lost souls.

"Onward Christian soldiers, marching as to war." Our voices announced our arrival outside the swinging doors of the rowdy taverns, Ogden Utah's main gates to hell.

The cacophony of our base drum, tuba, baritone, coronet, and tambourines battled with hillbilly music, drunken curses and raucous laughter blared from the bars.

Our music stopped. Captain Owens opened his bible.

"...keep yourselves in the love of God, looking for the mercy of our Lord Jesus Christ unto eternal life," he read aloud from his Holy Book. He then shouted out the call to salvation. "Come home to Jesus!"

Revelers drifted past like fish trapped in a relentless current. Some of the most drunk only maintained balance on their feet by bouncing from body to body. Many of the besotted were young Indians, whose bruised and pockmarked faces radiated a luminescent glow caused by the vast quantities of alcohol they consumed. With huge, drunken grins, a few paused momentarily in front of us. Some looked over the females in our group. Driven by their drinking demons, they quickly stumbled on to the next source of their beloved alcohol.

Drunks soaked in their own vomit sprawled on the sidewalk. More drunks leaned unsteadily against the dirty-brown brick buildings, and greedily took deep swallows from wine and whiskey bottles as they ignored our small group of Salvationists. We sang another hymn.

"Fucking Jesus lovers," a drunken voice shouted.

"Spread them for me, girly."

"Look at the big tits on the short one."

Virginia turned crimson. She sang louder. Al Davey bristled, but controlled himself. Peggy kept her eyes focused on her hymn book. My pretty stepsister didn't show any strong reaction to the wretchedness surrounding us. She appeared immune to the horrors we encountered as eager members of the Salvation Army. I wished I carried Al's fully loaded, thirty-aught-six rifle in my hands. I'd blast away the evil trying to swallow us up. The rest of the Salvationists concentrated on our mission of mercy.

Alcohol-sodden airmen, from nearby Hill Airbase, staggered from bar to bar. The stench of tobacco smoke, spilled beer, and misdirected urine flowed out of the saloons, wafted up from the sidewalks, and radiated from the constant flow of wasted humanity. Passing by us was a sea of distorted, battered, and time-ravaged faces. The worst of humanity was on vivid display and we willingly and eagerly marched into the morass.

Our instruments and our voices called out for repentance as we marched back across the street to continue the service inside our small chapel.

"With the cross of Jesus, going on before," our small band fervently sang.

Captain Owens held his gold-cross emblazoned Bible high over his head as he led us back in our house of worship. A few wobbly drunks followed us and slid in the pews furthest from the pulpit at the front. They reluctantly paid the price of listening to attempted salvation in order to earn free hot soup and buttered bread served after the service.

One dreary night, as we marched back in our church from Satan's street of hell, a young man, probably twenty-years-old, reeking of alcohol and with tears streaming down his flushed face, decided to follow us. I was fascinated by the sight and presence of him. Vibrating with what appeared to be insurmountable fear and anguish, he barely kept his balance through the service. Finally, the call for coming forward to salvation was sounded.

"For the grace of God that brings salvation has appeared to all men." Captain Owens intoned.

The young man forced himself to his feet. He paused in a moment of indecision. Gathering all his courage, he unsteadily made his way to the front railing below the pulpit where Captain Owens sermonized. Shaking visibly and shedding more tears, the young man knelt. To me, he appeared to be a person who lost every good thing life can offer. Delbert, the ever-ready, sympathizer-soldier, walked up and knelt beside him. Delbert put his hand on the young man's shoulder. He leaned in close to the young sufferer. He whispered prayers and comfort to the distraught sinner. The young man bowed his head. His whole body convulsed with sobs. My voice joined others in the assembly as we burst into song, and rejoiced over a potential, salvageable soul.

"Come home—come home.

Ye who are weary come home.

Harmlessly, tenderly Jesus is calling.

Calling all sinners, come home."

After the services ended, the young man ate hot soup and buttered bread. He listened to more words of comfort and encouragement from dedicated Salvationists. He slept in one of the cots made available upstairs for the alcoholic and homeless wanderers of the world.

The next evening, Mitch and I sat in the dining hall and talked. He'd sobered up, showered, and regained some of his pleasant, youthful face.

"She's so pretty. I love her so much. She said she loved me," Mitch recalled with a hopeful voice. "We talked about getting engaged. We talked about marriage. All our family members were going to attend our wedding. We promised each other we'd be together forever."

I remembered the girl I loved when I was seven-years-old and living with Rose and George in a gentle, small-town setting. I walked my love home from school and carried her books. We held each other's hands. My first love ended painfully. My pretty girl abandoned me for another boy.

Anger entered Mitch's voice and clouded his face. His display of anger made me uncomfortable.

"She changed. She said she wasn't sure if she was ready to settle down."

Tears formed in Mitch's eyes. I still sensed his anger. I didn't know what to say. I didn't understand the way he thought and talked. I already understood loving people was dangerous. You never knew when they wouldn't love you anymore and how mean they'd turn out to really be. You never knew when they'd walk away and leave you. After my mother made a habit of abandoning me, I always imagined the most devastating possibilities in life. Why wasn't Mitch ready for the inevitable?

"She's very close to her family. I suspect they didn't think I was good enough for her. I'm an honest person, Mickey. I'm a good person."

Mitch looked at me for confirmation.

"I think you're a good guy." I wasn't really telling the truth. The undercurrent of constant anger in Mitch scared me. Maybe his anger scared his girlfriend.

"I struggled through school. I couldn't please my family. I wasn't making enough money in my job. I couldn't satisfy my boss. I couldn't fulfill anyone's expectations of me."

Weighed down by his failures, Mitch's shoulders sagged. He sounded like a convicted murderer who stood under the hangman's noose and tearfully pleaded for a second chance at life.

"I'm praying she'll take me back. I don't want to return to the horrible drinking life on skid row. I didn't know what else to do. The thought of losing her hurt so much."

"I'll pray for you Mitch." What the hell was I doing? Why was I listening to someone else's problems? I wasn't close to being a whole person myself. I didn't feel much hope for my own future.

. . .

Within a few days, Mitch completely sobered up. He appeared strong enough to face his future. Maybe his girlfriend would take him back. Maybe she'd salvage his life. But, he needed to deal with the possibility of love's end. From Captain Owens office, he made a phone call. He hoped the call would resurrect his dreams.

I stood outside the office. I heard distress grow in Mitch's pleading voice. The phone clunked down loudly onto the receiver.

Mitch stumbled out of the office. He held his hands over his face. He cried out, "She says it's over forever!"

He ran out the front door of the center.

I ran after him. I watched him careen down the skid row street.

"Mitch!" I called after him. "Mitch!"

He staggered along the filthy sidewalk. He clawed at his face and screamed. He was being sucked into the terrible black-ness of despair. He disappeared in the merciless shadows of skid row.

I walked back in the chapel and sat in a pew. I grieved for Mitch. I grieved for myself. I knew too well the place he'd been cast in.

I looked up at the photograph of Jesus on the wall. Jesus looked down at me with love. I remembered. I was safe. I forced myself back from the edge of the abyss.

As I walked out of the chapel, a surge of relief flowed through me. I was glad Mitch disappeared in the unknown. I hoped I wouldn't ever see him again. I didn't need another reminder of the further horrors life might bring to me.

CHAPTER THIRTEEN

I listened to sermons and silently mouthed hymns at the Salvation Army services. What I heard most clearly was Jesus loved the lowest of humanity. Jesus loved the leper, the crippled, the weak, the old, the ugly. Above all, Jesus loved the unloved.

Was Jesus my only chance of ever finding true, unconditional love?

Jesus grew to a heroic figure in my eyes. His father God was a pretty rough character, always in a fury and punishing people. I didn't need any more punishment. I had a totally different picture of his son. Jesus always smiled, always loved and was kind, except when he got mad at the moneychangers in the temple. More than anything, I appreciated Jesus was gentle.

I read a pamphlet that quoted words from the scriptures. "Through the Lord's mercies we are not consumed, because His compassions fail not."

. . .

After many times stopping myself from rising from my seat and stepping forward, I finally answered the call to salvation. I forced myself to my feet. I walked up to the railing below the pulpit. I knelt and bowed my head. I recklessly exposed myself to strangers. I couldn't stem the flow of tears from my eyes.

"Yes," I prayed. "Jesus, please help me."

I trembled with hope and fear. I sensed Delbert walking up behind me. I felt his heavy presence kneel beside me. He put his arm around my shoulders. I flinched. He gripped me tighter. He whispered prayers in my ear. I didn't like his body smell. I didn't like the staleness of his breath. Most of all, I hated when he touched me. It took great effort to not pull away from him, stand, and run from the chapel as fast as I could move.

After several minutes, I stood. Everyone witnessed me trembling and sobbing. I opened myself up to everyone. How could I? Did I really believe in what I just did? Was I a sniveling traitor to the demon inside of me that really wanted murderous revenge against every one of our enemies? Was I deceiving everyone who thought my salvation was sincere? I still didn't trust any living person. How could I trust this dead Jesus?

There was much attention to and rejoicing over my having surrendered to the Lord. Worshippers gathered around me. I heard voices say, "This boy found Jesus." Virginia hugged me and kissed me on the cheek. I wanted to scream. I wanted to flee this new life I recklessly stumbled in. But, like a sniveling coward, I forced myself to act out the entire charade. At least I could use this redemption, true or false, as my armor against Mormon intolerance. I could hide behind my new religious fervor.

"Yes, we will gather at the river-

The beautiful, the beautiful river.
Gather with the saints at the river-
That flows by the throne of God!"

A couple of kids from school walked along skid row looking for evil entertainment. They saw me in my Salvation Army uniform at the curbside services as I helped with the call for salvation. They stopped, gawked, pointed, and laughed. I silently wished them an eternity in hell.

I dreaded going to school the next day more than usual.

"The retard was out on skid row singing to the drunks."

"Hey, you idiot. Why don't you wear your stupid uniform to school?"

"He can't wear his stupid uniform to school because a couple of skid row drunks puked all over him."

The story spread throughout the school and the target on my back grew even larger.

In a building located close to Lewis Junior High, the Mormons held an hour of religious study before the start of public school academic classes. From listening to fellow Salvationists, I learned Mormons are the only so-called Christian religion that believes in a prophet who came after Jesus. Mormons believe Joseph Smith was sent revelations from God, which he wrote down in the book of Mormon. Mormons believe the only path to heaven is through baptism in the Mormon Church.

The enthusiasm of that teaching carried over to my home-room. The students talked excitedly about Mormonism and the wonders of the Book of Mormon.

I made a big mistake. I took my conversion to Jesus Christ too seriously.

"The Bible is the only true book of God and Jesus," I said to a student who sat next to me. My voice was loud enough to be heard throughout the classroom. I didn't have any academic knowledge to back up my statement. I relied on the superficial teachings of my new religion. Those teachings clearly stated false prophets, and false scriptures were the worst of sins.

A moment of deathly silence followed my careless words.

The red-faced teacher spoke up. "You apologize immediately, Shafer."

Unsure of what was happening, I stared at her. Then, the memory of Naomi kicking me while I cowered on the ground like a frightened dog scorched my brain. An uncontrollable defiance welled up in me. A blind stubbornness possessed me. Beyond my control, my voice repeated those words.

"The Bible is the only true book of God and Jesus."

The teacher's face flushed with fury.

I wanted to retreat, but the demon inside of me took control of my mind. The demon wouldn't let me back down or flee from this deadly danger. The demon wanted all-out, scorched-earth war.

My classmates boiled in a rage.

"Don't talk about my religion that way," a delicate-faced girl said. Tears formed in her blue eyes.

An explosion of angry voices surrounded me. The demon wouldn't be dissuaded.

"Read the Holy Bible," I insisted.

"You're a liar. You're a terrible liar."

"Joseph Smith is a true Prophet."

"The Book of Mormon is the truest word."

The teacher glared at me with deep anger. "You're a terrible person, Shafer."

She spoke directly to the class, "What are you children going to do about this attack on our religion?" Crimson-faced, she turned and strode out of the classroom. I heard the door lock behind her. I sat at my desk like a convicted killer strapped in the electric chair. The storm around me erupted into a hurricane.

"You're ignorant."

"You're stupid white trash."

"You're worse than a nigger."

"You're worse than a Catholic."

"You're worse than a Jew."

"You're worse than a filthy, redskin savage."

My fellow students pelted me with pencils, rubber erasers, pens. As a mob, they stood and closed in on me. Spit cascaded down on me. I sat rigid and silent. I stared at my bloodless, white hands gripping the edges of my desk. After nightmarish abuse and total abandonment by my father, multiple abandonments by my mother, and the horror of Naomi, I believed I could bear any punishment.

"You're a son-of-a-bitch." Hard kicks punished my legs.

"You're an ignorant skid row bum." Fists pummeled my arms and shoulders.

I told myself I could suffer like Jesus suffered. I believed in him. Unlike Jesus, I felt hate. I wanted to strike back at my enemies. I wanted to kill my enemies. I also wanted to survive.

Everyone joined in the assault except the Black girl in our class. She glanced sideways at me with fear and disbelief showing clearly in her eyes. It looked like she wanted to flee, but she was frozen in terror. This attack might turn in her direction. She was the only Black person who attended this school and the Mormons didn't like Blacks any more than my family in Chicago and Indiana. I'd overheard my classmates quote the writings of Brigham Young. "Cain slew his brother. And the Lord put a mark upon him, which is the flat nose and black skin." This Black girl bore both marks.

After several minutes, the door was unlocked from the outside. The teacher returned. She gave me another hateful look. She then ignored my existence as the class quietly returned to scholarly pursuits.

CHAPTER FOURTEEN

My alienation from my Mormon classmates continued absolute and without mercy. I sensed deeply the danger I was in among these followers of Joseph Smith. With my words and actions, I branded myself a hell-bound heretic. The teachings of their church condemned me to eternal damnation. To survive in this Latter-Day Saint world, I needed to keep my mouth shut. I needed to stay as invisible as possible.

I read the Bible searching for answers.

"Blessed are they which are persecuted for righteousness' sake: for theirs is the kingdom of Heaven.

Blessed are ye, when men shall revile you, and persecute you, and shall say all manner of evil against you falsely, for my sake.

Rejoice, and be exceeding glad: for great is your reward in Heaven: for so persecuted they the prophets which were before you." Saint Matthew 5.10-12

From the Bible, I learned my religious persecution wasn't unique. I belonged to a brotherhood of long deceased martyrs.

I memorized the first doctrine of the Salvation Army:

"We believe that the Scriptures of the Old and New Testaments were given by inspiration of God, and only they constitute the Divine rule of Christian faith and practice."

For me, this was indisputable evidence Mormons weren't true Christians. My suffering at their hands would be noble and blessed by God.

Word of my presence, a voice exposing Mormon heresy, spread throughout the school. I unleashed a maelstrom upon myself from which there was no escape.

The continuing punishment was both verbal and physical. My banishment from the cultish Mormon society was absolute.

Just like she responded to most of life's challenges, Peggy stayed quiet and reserved in her involvement with religion. She showed extreme caution in her interactions with Mormons. She showed extreme caution in her interactions with me. I knew she didn't understand the kind of human I was. She didn't know about the raging demons driving me. She knew nothing of the horrid circumstances of my slavery to Naomi. Sometimes, I thought she viewed me like a dog that couldn't ever learn to quit chasing cars, and just like one of those crazy mutts, I was destined to be run over by a speeding delivery truck and killed.

Aloofness appeared to be her safety net. She walked to school by herself and avoided me during the school day. At school, we lived in two separate worlds that couldn't be shared. Despite her prettiness and pleasantness, she was also cruelly ostracized by the Mormons. The Mormons showed no mercy on any outsiders, but because she never voiced her opinions about religion, she was not hated by them to the intensity I was.

At home, she gave me some recognition as a living person. I appreciated any tiny morsel of attention I got from her. But, I was still an alien in her world. I submissively acted out my role as an out-of-place interloper in my mother's new family. I watched my stepsister, Peggy, go about her daily activities. I lived out my fantasies of unattainable love. Still, her living presence made my life more bearable. Watching her body movements, her interacting with the world, and her silent, contemplative existence, gave me a much needed glimpse of a normal, functioning human.

She never put it in words, but her every action stated: "You're on your own, Mickey. You have to watch out for yourself. I can't help you."

The required Physical Education class at school was one of my worst punishments to be endured.

I half-heartedly attempted to play baseball. My mind and body refused to cooperate. The angry demon inside of me rebelled against any expectations imposed by outside forces. He didn't like to be told what to do. He despised the effort and concentration required in a game like baseball. The demon considered all of it nothing more than submission to higher powers who were brutal dictators. "Don't order me about," the demon screamed. Resist, resist, resist was his mantra.

Assigned the position where I could cause the least damage, I stood in the outfield. I listened to the crack of the bat against the ball. It's not coming my way. Thank you, God. Again, I heard the crack of the bat against the ball. The ball was coming my way. I watched the tiny white sphere. How far was it going to go? How soon would it reach me? Was it going to fly beyond me? Was it going to fall short of where I stood frozen in my tracks? Would it hit me in my face? It looked like it's going to my right. How far to my right would it go? I staggered in that direction. My feet tangled in the short grass. I reached out with my gloved hand. The ball fell several feet away from me. I struggled to pick it up. Finally, I held the stupid ball in my hand. I threw the stupid ball. It went only half as far and ten feet to the left of where it needed to go.

"What a spastic!" The chorus from competent athletes resounded. "Catch the ball, stupid."

I didn't care. The demon inside me cheered my indifference to failure.

I shut down my emotions. I hid behind a wall of indifference. If I had a choice, I'd live in my own fantasy world where I'd be totally alone. I'd be totally free from the presence of all humans. I did sometimes think I'd like to have my lovely stepsister, Peggy, join me in my wonderful world of isolation. It'd also be nice to have a rifle, lots of ammunition, and a loyal dog.

I arrived home after another day of hellish harassment at school. Virginia was entertaining two women from the Mormon Relief Society's "visiting teaching" program. Shrouded in total devotion to their church, those two women clutched and read from their Bibles and Book of Mormon. Virginia listened courteously, but she visibly struggled to fulfill the role of a gracious hostess. The two devotees looked up and smiled at me as I tried to ease past them unnoticed.

"This is my son, Mickey," Virginia said brightly.

"Hello, Mickey," The two saints chorused.

"Hi."

"How was school, Mickey?" Virginia asked with a motherly smile.

"School was okay."

"We have such fine schools here," one of the Mormon women intoned. "Our children are so well behaved. They're filled with kindness and overflowing with love."

"It must be so much nicer living in Ogden than it was in a sinful city like Chicago," the other Mormon declared.

"It kind of is." I forced a smile, turned away, walked on, and made my escape.

Virginia was stuck with her visitors. I knew she really wanted friends who drank coffee, smoked cigarettes, and laughed with her. Mormons didn't commit those sins.

Why did she attempt to socialize with these Latter Day Saint women? I guess she was trapped by her need to be courteous to everyone. Her years of working as a waitress and always smiling at customers were hard to overcome. The Mormon's goal was to convert her to the only correct way of life, Mormonism. I overheard some of our fellow Salvationists say Joseph Smith was a treasure-hunting charlatan. He was a joke to them. He was a laughable prophet.

Of course, none of the Salvationists said out loud what they really believed. Only I was so naive and stupid. Offering no guidance and warnings, my fellow Salvationists let me foolishly stumble in the inferno. Would I have recklessly rushed in the flames anyway? Would the demon force me to do his bidding, and make me stubbornly fight against everyone and everything?

CHAPTER FIFTEEN

From my castaway's cot in the hallway, I was forced to hear Al and Virginia in their room at night.

"Come on," Al pleaded.

"I don't want to," she protested. "You're too hairy. You stink like a bear. You need to take a shower."

"I always take a shower in the morning."

"Quit it. I don't want to."

"Please."

"No."

"Please, Virginia."

"Okay. Damn it."

I heard their bed groan as he climbed on top of her. I listened to him grunt. Damn. He sounded like a bear. He grunted louder. He grunted faster. The bed springs screamed for several seconds. The noises blended together like a deadly collision of a thousand automobiles. Sudden silence startled me. He let out a big sigh. He groaned like he was dying.

"Get off of me," she ordered. Her voice dripped with hate.

This disgusting event didn't take place often, but when it

did, I covered my head with my pillow. The muted sounds still burrowed in my brain. I wanted to erase the sickening scene completely from my mind, but I couldn't. I despised and pitied both of them.

I despised myself when the same awful sickness surged through me. Thankfully, Peggy didn't know about the self-centered and unrestrained depths I sunk to when I was alone. I knew she wouldn't ever participate in that loathsome, grunting activity. She was a crystalline-pure mountain stream, gently flowing past a sweetly-fragrant field of blue and yellow flowers.

Al Davey worked for the Union Pacific Railroad for twenty-one years. He planned to work for them until he reached retirement age. His job in the tool crib at the repair yard wasn't highly skilled or highly paid, but his railroad career was the greatest prize in his life.

The money they sent for my train fare from Chicago to Ogden was a hard hit on their tight budget. I knew Virginia didn't want me returned to her and didn't want me to be a part of her new life, but here I was, adding to their already strained food budget. I was a burden they weren't prepared for. I was dumped on them.

Virginia talked at me when we were alone. She conveniently omitted any mention of the part where she gave me to Naomi and how she disposed of my brothers. It was all about her. She explained her flight from Chicago landed her in Waverly, Colorado, jobless and penniless. She met Al when she answered an ad for a housekeeper and nanny. Al Davey's beloved country-wife died, leaving him wifeless and his young daughter, Peggy, motherless. Of course, soon after Virginia went to work for him, Al fell in love with her. For some crazy reason, she married this older man who worked for the Union

Pacific railroad at a low-paying job. They lived on his rundown farm on the outskirts of a terribly boring and dying little Colorado town.

Damn her! If she hadn't given me away to Naomi, she could've brought me out West with her. She and I could've been together. Any kind of life with her would've been better than being Naomi's punching bag and slave.

My mother was born with an incurable case of wanderlust. Free from all five sons she gave birth to, she traveled out to the wild-west in search of adventure and fortune. She ended up as Al Davey's hired housekeeper.

I sensed her seething hatred for him because of the humiliation of having been his servant. Yet, she married him. I knew he was far from the ideal man for her. If she couldn't have the pot of gold at the end of the rainbow, at least she needed a thrilling thunderstorm. Al meant well, but he hovered about her like a low-hanging, black cloud.

She developed a strong affection for her new stepdaughter, Peggy. It was a much stronger affection than she maintained towards any of her own sons.

The Union Pacific transferred Al from Waverly, Colorado to Ogden, Utah. They left his patch-of-dirt farm behind. Virginia was glad to be rid of the dirty, noisy chickens, and the stone-age plumbing. Even living among proselytizing Mormons was better than the isolation of a decrepit mini-ranch in the middle of nowhere.

Occasionally, after Sunday morning services, we went to Delbert's for lunch. Delbert, Ida, and their eight-year-old, hyperactive, adopted son lived in a singlewide mobile home. The living room, which we all squeezed in, became the dining room, when a foldaway table was lowered from the wall. Inches past the tiny kitchen were two bunk beds and the narrow passageway that led to the single bathroom and master bedroom. Delbert and Ida were large people and I marveled they were able to live in such a small space. Their red-haired, freckled-faced, adopted kid never stopped moving and talking.

A small black and white television sat on a shelf in the living room. Seven of us crowded together to watch a popular evangelist sermonize and heal the lame and sick. The tent where he performed his miracles was as large as any circus tent I ever saw. People of every color and age filled his canvas auditorium to capacity. Worshipper's bodies and voices vibrated with passion as a procession of suffering souls stood and tottered down the aisles to be touched and healed. The son of God reached out through the hands of his earthly vessel, the miracle worker, Oral Roberts.

Oral grasped the heads of the hopelessly ill and lame with his strong hands.

"Through the power of Jesus!" he shouted. "Heal this poor sinner."

The miracle seeking bodies shuddered and vibrated. The desperate raised their trembling hands to God. Electricity appeared to flow from Jesus Christ in heaven, through red-faced, perspiring Oral Roberts, and entered the ravaged bodies of people seeking restoration of youthful health.

Cripples who couldn't walk to the front without leaning on crutches were healed. They cast aside their crutches and demonstrated to the audience that they now walked freely.

"Hallelujah!" Oral shouted as he raised his hands to the heavens. "Praise the Lord!" Sweat glistened on Oral's brow. Oral's face lit up as a bright light beamed down from heaven, radiated off him, and spread over the audience.

"Hallelujah!" The crowd echoed.

Both the healed and unhealed shed tears.

"Hallelujah," Oral shouted. He placed his hands on another sufferer's head. The person vibrated from head to toe. Overcome with the healing power, they fell backwards in the waiting arms of Oral's assistants.

I watched with awe as Oral preached and performed his miracles. I waited for the delicious lunch Ida prepared in her limited kitchen space. I thought it was a mighty fine miracle we all fit in the cramped, little trailer. Another miracle was not bumping elbows as we crowded up to the small dining table and wielded our silverware. In these tight quarters, I prayed I'd sit next to my lovely stepsister, Peggy. Miraculously, I did. Crowded next to each other, I felt the heat of her body. Our legs touched. I bumped her bare arm with my bare arm. I felt her wonderful skin against mine. My penis stirred from its slumber. I fulfilled the ultimate desire of my wretched life. I knew I was terribly sinful. I hoped Jesus wasn't watching me and didn't realize what I was getting away with. I prayed Jesus couldn't read my mind and didn't know how sinful my thoughts were.

CHAPTER SIXTEEN

During my first winter in Utah, I went hunting with Al Davey. I didn't have a license or rifle, but he was satisfied with my company. A hunter trekking off in the wilderness totally alone was always risky. My walking gait may have been a bit odd, but I now wore boots that fit and could walk fast and far. I didn't feel a need to talk. Stalking deer and idle chatter didn't mix. A skilled deer hunter, Al owned a Springfield, .30-06, semi-automatic rifle. Unlike many hunters, he didn't need to spend money on a telescopic sight. He used the rear and front sight the rifle came with. Rock steady and deadly accurate, he didn't miss his target when he shot. Bullets cost money and being poor, he counted every penny he spent.

Al took Virginia hunting with him early in their relationship and it turned out disastrously. She looked forward to a pleasant visit with nature. Instead, it was a relentless trek through thick sagebrush and hard climbs up rock strewn mountainsides. In this setting, Al didn't grovel before her. Instead, he impatiently drove her to keep pace with him. That unpleasant experience was yet another reason for her to hate him.

Al's young daughter, Peggy, didn't have any interest in hiking through wilderness to kill and gut beautiful, harmless deer.

Al and I left the house in four-in-the-morning darkness and bone-chilling cold. We drove twelve miles up through Ogden Canyon. The ice littered Ogden River, which nourished many cottonwood trees along its banks, flowed roughly on our right. We turned off the main highway and crept and slid a couple of miles down a pot-holed, dirt side-road. The cumbersome Pontiac automobile struggled across the sloppy, snowy slush layered over hard frozen ice. Eventually, we found a safe place to park.

Al carried his rifle and I carried our lunch and his thermos of coffee. We hurriedly hiked a couple of miles uphill from the road. We were in quiet wilderness as a new day was born and were blessed with a beautiful sunrise breaking through the morning mist. I loved the rich early-morning smells of sage-brush and moist earth.

At a crystal-clear stream, we broke through a thin layer of ice and drank handfuls of ice-cold water. We analyzed the visible tracks of the wide array of wildlife that shared this price-less refreshment. The hoof prints of many deer in the water's muddy edge gave us high hopes for success in our hunt.

Al was a restless hunter. We were always on the move and hiked for miles through the beautiful Wasatch Mountains. As we climbed, we stepped carefully over sharp-edged rocks and loose shale. We kept our noise to a minimum. We traversed ridges covered with pungent smelling sagebrush, rabbit brush, and prickly juniper. I never tired of the wonderful aromas of the pristine wilderness. As we trekked, I saw where grazing wildlife pawed through the thin layer of ice to get at sparse grass. When we reached the top of a mountain, we stopped for a few moments to rest among groves of fir, spruce pine, and aspen trees.

My elation at reaching unspoiled nature at the top of a mountain was a great reward for the strenuous effort of the ascent. I liked to imagine we were the first humans to ever step onto a particular patch of ground.

It was a dramatic change going from the small patches of snow on the sunny side of the peaks, to a heavy accumulation on the shaded side. As we struggled through knee-deep drifts of cold, white powder, I envied how the deer easily bounded through the same obstacle.

Al wanted to stay clear of the majority of other hunters. Many of those preferred to find a spot on a ridge halfway up a mountain. They sat and waited for the deer to come to them. Some hunters drank too much whiskey and thought any movement they saw across a canyon was a big buck. There always existed the possibility of being hit by a fool's bullet.

We searched for fresh signs as we followed the narrow paths created by the deer. Recent droppings of feces kept us extra alert and if we happened upon a steaming pile, we halted to look and listen. A big buck might be nearby and standing motionless as he listened to us. Hopefully our prey would move first and reveal his location. If the deer decided to flee, they bounded away and were usually out of range before a hunter could react.

The mule deer of Utah were plentiful and large. The opening of deer-hunting season brought the tramp of many human feet in areas where they usually weren't heard at all. The booming of high-powered rifles destroyed any illusion of a wilderness sanctuary. Despite the thrill of the hunt, I felt remorse I was part of the merciless onslaught. The deer had more than hunters to worry about. They needed to be alert for hunger-driven mountain lions.

I looked forward to lunchtime. I couldn't stomach the sandwiches of potted meat with mayonnaise on white bread Al preferred. That canned meat was awful stuff. I always insisted on luncheon meat and sliced cheese with mustard on white bread. After a few hours of difficult hiking over miles of treacherous terrain, the sandwiches tasted as delicious as anything I ever ate. Al still ate those damn potted meat sandwiches he took to work every day in his black, metal lunchbox. Jesus Christ. Yuck!

We shared his thermos of hot coffee which contained lots of sugar and cream.

It might take several weekends, but eventually we killed our deer. The winter's meat supply was butchered, wrapped, labeled, frozen, and stored in a rented meat locker. The novelty of venison roasts, steaks, chops and burgers faded after a month or so, but money was tight and we ate on. Real beef, pork, or poultry was a welcome, but expensive treat.

CHAPTER SEVENTEEN

Jamie Lopez, a fellow soldier at the Salvation Army who was also thirteen-years-old, stood five-foot-nine and weighed around a hundred-fifty-pounds. I was five-foot-six and weighed maybe a hundred pounds at most.

"You're always walking around with your eyes on the ground, Mickey," Jamie chastised me. "You act like you're afraid of everything. Be proud, Mickey. Hold your head high."

He made a good observation. He gave me advice I remembered. I just needed to find the courage to follow his well-intentioned words.

Jamie and I went camping in the wilderness for a weekend. His father, who spoke only Spanish, gave us a ride to the trailhead. Jamie seemed uncomfortable with his father's lack of English and servile demeanor. Mexicans were not well regarded by most whites in Utah and the Mormons were even more hateful in their prejudice.

After a friendly handshake from Mr. Lopez, Jamie and I hiked uphill under a sky filled with threatening, dark clouds. We located a good camping spot next to a fast-flowing, crystal-clear stream. The gray mist that enveloped both us and the surrounding wilderness quickly turned to a soaking rain. We hurriedly set up our tent.

Rain fell for the two days and one night we camped. We spent most of our time inside the tent, leaving the front flap open only when less violent winds and downpours allowed. We both crowded at the small opening to look out at the lousy weather washing away any hope of exploration and adventure. We ate our hot dogs we planned to roast over an open camp fire uncooked, and the pork and beans, cold out of the can. If nature called, it was off behind some bush we rushed. The rain didn't have the courtesy of pausing.

"Don't use all the toilet paper."

"You sure snore too loud."

"One of us should have checked the weather forecast."

"Don't you ever quit complaining?"

"Why don't you go outside to fart?"

"Jesus must really be pissed at me!"

Waterlogged and weary, we trudged back to the trailhead to meet Jamie's father at the prearranged time. By then, we were completely irritated and totally bored with each other.

It hadn't been what you'd call a super-close friendship anyway.

A few days after the camping trip, my stepsister, Peggy, and I walked side by side along the sidewalk. She was tall and lovely next to me. We bumped hands. An electrical charge like the one that made Frankenstein the Monster take his first breath surged through my body. I was alive! I existed!

Two preppy looking boys, conversing and snickering, strode cockily towards us. Both looked to be a couple of years older and at least forty pounds heavier than me. This time, I didn't lower my eyes in an attempt to hide. I needed to be brave in front of Peggy. She needed my protection. I looked them in the eye as they approached. When they got next to us, I saw a blur of movement.

"What the fuck you looking at freak?"

A hard fist landed square on my face. A spectacular display of streaky colors and bizarre shapes flashed across my vision. Completely stunned, I fell to my knees. Blood erupted from my nose and swamped my mouth. Nausea overwhelmed me. I crumpled onto the concrete and curled in a fetal position. Goddamn, I hated the taste of my own warm blood.

"You lousy bastards," Peggy screamed at the grinning thugs as they jauntily walked on.

They looked back at us and laughed mockingly. They held up their middle fingers as a crude rebuke. They postured with a threat to return and deliver more punishment.

I lay helpless on the sidewalk. I held my hand against my throbbing nose to stem the red flow.

"Are you okay, Mickey?" She knelt next to me and placed her hand on my shoulder.

I couldn't speak. My lovely stepsister, Peggy, cared enough to ask about my well being. I should've been terribly ashamed to have her see me as a sniveling coward, lying helpless on the sidewalk. Her hand remained on my shoulder. She offered me her neckerchief to wipe away my blood. I hated myself for relishing her sympathy. I loved her more than ever, if possible. I would happily bleed to death to keep her close, feel her breath, and have her hands continue touching me.

. . .

That night, I lay on my hallway cot a few feet from the door to her room. I dreamed. It wasn't the dream I wanted of her and I holding each other close.

A pallid shell overlaid with putrid scabs staggered and stumbled aimlessly. The person imprisoned inside the shell couldn't see the condition of their exterior body. With increasing desperation, they looked out through a small hole in their shell. The world and its people reacted to them with disgust and fear. Once smiling faces were now twisted with distaste. Many cursed the shell. Many spit on the shell. Mobs gathered and stoned the shell. The shell didn't break in a million fragments. Instead, the shell grew thicker. The rage inside the shell magnified with each abuse. The person inside the shell cursed with his loudest voice and vilest words.

The shell didn't explode like a deadly nuclear bomb and destroy every last one of the enemy. The person inside the shell burst in flames from the heat of their own rage. The person inside the shell burned until only gray ashes remained. The shell collapsed inward and shriveled to a rotten little lump. The sordid little mess was buried under billions and billions of tons of human waste. The shell and its occupant were forgotten, as if never having existed.

The next day I sat at my desk as the classroom emptied. Two boys lingered at the front. They conversed and watched me. When I was finally ready to make my escape, I stood. One of the boys pointed at me. He balled up his fist. He nudged his friend. It appeared he was urging his buddy to take me on in a fistfight.

Words drifted over to me. "He's easy." The one being urged

to fight clenched his hands in fists and held them chest high. Both of my fair-haired, clean-faced classmates looked confident of victory.

"Come on retard. I'm going to kick your ass," the designated bully challenged me. He had an innocent grin on his face. I didn't see one hint of toughness or meanness in his expression.

Rage boiled up and overwhelmed me. I rushed forward, my fists ready. I aimed for his face. He didn't lift his hands to deflect my punches. He didn't have a clue. I hit him in the face three times before he finally lowered his head and covered up with his arms.

"Quit hitting me," he cried.

Ecstatic at the sensation of inflicting injury to the flesh of a tormentor, I hit him twice more on the side of his head, close to his ears. I couldn't pass up such an easy target. The instigator, with a look of shock across his face, turned and fled from the classroom. I stopped swinging. A bruise was rapidly developing next to my challenger's eye. Blood dribbled from his nose. The tearful, baby-faced bully, struggling to understand what happened, turned and ran out of the classroom. I felt sorry for the fool. Obviously, he hadn't ever boxed with intent to hurt someone or been hit in the face by an angry fist.

No teachers or other authority figures rushed to the classroom to take control of me, the brutal thug.

After that incident, only the bigger jock types bullied me. For them, I remained a despised and easy victim.

Looking just like the hell I visualized from the Holy Bible, Lewis Junior High school turned to a real inferno. The fire took place on a dark, freezing-cold night. Al, Virginia, Peggy, and I bundled up and joined a crowd of other onlookers. We watched as the two-story structure was consumed by a tornado of relentless flames.

The polishing-wax soaked wood floors, wood doors, wood window frames, and wood desks provided potent fuel that burned outrageously hot. It was a spectacular blaze. Dense smoke and brilliant showers of sparks rose in the black, night sky. Away from the intense heat, massive icicles formed from the large volume of water sprayed by many fire hoses. When the final embers were extinguished, only a hollow, brick shell filled with fantastic formations of ice was left. It looked as if the hands of a brilliant sculptor had been at work and created an unearthly masterpiece. The caustic smell of charred wood wasn't as pleasant as the visuals of the fire's destruction.

I always enjoyed watching the largest building fires in Chicago. Watching Lewis Junior High School go up in flames was one of the most satisfying structure fires I ever witnessed.

CHAPTER EIGHTEEN

The students from Lewis Junior High were transferred to Ogden High School. Most of us were Lilliputians amongst giants. My walking distance to school doubled. Although Lewis Junior High School's interior was turned to ashes, bad memories of that hellhole lingered and festered in my mind.

My person was inconsequential, but my crime against the Mormon religion was of great enormity. My notoriety preceded me to Ogden High School.

I was an ignorant, non-believer. I was a blasphemer who dared to challenge the legitimacy of the prophet Joseph Smith and the truth of his writings. I insulted The Book of Mormon.

Don't look anyone in the eye. It's an invitation to a hard-knuckled fist.

"Who're you looking at retard? You want to get your ass kicked."

The tight spasm of fear hit my sphincter. My testicles shriveled up and tried to hide inside my body.

"Pant's him!"

The mob converged. They grabbed me and threw me to the ground. Rough hands unbuckled my belt, unzipped my fly, grabbed the legs of my pants and pulled. I twisted and I kicked, but to no avail. The mob was relentless and powerful. Laughing faces, grabbing hands and surrounding bodies blocked out the sky and the sun. My trousers were below my knees. Hands with ragged fingernails grabbed and pulled down my underwear. My terrified penis shriveled up more and hid further in my skinny body.

"Look at his ugly dick!"

Mocking faces stared down at my pale-white body. My cowardly penis continued its retreat. There wasn't anywhere for the rest of me to hide.

They released me. I frantically pulled up my undershorts and my grass-stained pants.

"The retard has an ugly little dick!"

With my head bowed, I crouched and shuffled away, looking at no one.

Fingers pointed, faces twisted in glee. The mob screamed and howled abuse.

Day after day, I ran the gauntlet.

Jesus hung naked and helpless on the cross. Jesus bled and suffered terrible pain. I should have been able to cringe naked on the ground.

Unlike forgiving Jesus, I wanted to kill each and every member of the mob. If only I possessed the power to kill.

Throw a punch and flinch was a favorite game of boys my age. I played the game many times with my older brothers, Tommy and Ben. They weren't bashful or restrained when they hit me.

They had the right to hit me whenever and as hard as they wanted because they were my older brothers.

Real punches and threatened punches were a constant now from kids I hated and feared. I never knew where the next hit would come from, or what part of my body the fist would hit. It might be a quick fist to my stomach, or my arm, or my back. Some were definitely meant to hurt, while others came just close enough to elicit a flinch.

Punch.

Flinch.

Dodge a punch.

Stumble in avoiding the swing.

Flinching was now a constant of my life.

If only I possessed the power to kill each and every one of the punchers.

CHAPTER NINETEEN

Virginia wanted to make the 750-mile drive from dreary Ogden to exciting Los Angeles for our summer vacation.

"I don't think it's a good idea," Al objected. Once again, he wasn't thinking of the dangerous ground he walked. "I don't think we can afford a trip like that."

He worried his beloved 1948 Pontiac wouldn't hold up across the many miles of hot desert between us and the beautiful coast of California. Seven years and ninety-thousand-miles of rough roads took its toll on the heavy-bodied sedan. Virginia gave him a scathing look of impatience.

"The car will be fine," she said. "Let's have some fun for a change."

It was obvious from her expression and tone of voice she was thinking, "Damn Al and his boring, cautious nature."

Al reacted with both hurt and submission.

I thought a trip in the car was a fabulous idea. Peggy usually stayed aloof and kept a physical distance between us. On an auto journey, she'd be stuck in the back seat with me for the entire 1,500-mile round trip to California. I'd be close to her twenty-four-hours a day, for eight glorious days.

I was thirteen. She was fourteen. So, what she'd gotten prettier by the day? It wasn't my fault I remained a pale, scrawny introvert. What the hell. I recently won a bloody fist-fight at school.

Virginia easily got her way. Quickly, we prepared for our eight-day road-trip to magical California.

We drove southwest on Route 91, a major two-lane U.S. highway traversing the length of Utah. After she made Al give in and accept the challenge of this adventure, he didn't seem to mind being on the road. The only licensed driver among us, his level of importance rose considerably. Virginia seemed momentarily satisfied, so he probably thought he gained in her affection. He chain smoked Pall Malls as the rest of us kept our faces close to the partially open car windows to breathe in the cleaner outside air. Virginia was once again attempting to kick her smoking habit.

"Do you have to smoke so much, Al?"

His face appeared apologetic, but it was highly unlikely he'd ever slow down his chain smoking, or permanently give up his cherished Pall Malls.

The man and the woman in the front seat of the automobile were married, but barely spoke to each other. I saw it as terribly depressing, one-way-love in action. Al worshipped her, and Virginia struggled to tolerate him.

In the backseat, Peggy and I, who were thrown together solely by a twist of fate, kept our distance from each other. Our relationship remained a heartbreaking, one-way-love. I adored her, and wanted to believe she didn't absolutely dismiss me from her thoughts.

We cruised along the precisely laid out streets of Salt Lake City. The immaculate metropolis was dominated by the white-marble beauty of the towering Mormon Temple. A gold leafed statue of the angel Moroni topped the highest of the six steeples of the massive, religious edifice. The angel Moroni spoke to Joseph Smith and led him to the golden plates which Joseph translated into the Book of Mormon. Even though I prayed to the same God, Mormons claim only those who are baptized as Mormons would be allowed entry to the paradise of heaven. What a crazy idea. Hell was going to be very crowded.

"The Mormons certainly built a beautiful city," Virginia observed. "And they keep it spotlessly clean."

"It's a clean place, but you'll never be liked in Utah unless you belong to their religion," Peggy lamented.

"Don't worry, Peggy," Virginia turned back and gave her a reassuring smile. "They'll love you in California. They'll love you everywhere else in the world. Once you leave Utah, you won't have to worry about Mormons."

Peggy and I both suffered harsh punishment for not being Latter Day Saints. She was shunned. My punishment was a thousand times multiplied because I hadn't kept my mouth shut about false prophets and scriptures, the supposed blasphemy whispered about among the Salvationists, and many other Non-Mormons. Much wiser than I, those gossipers knew better than to express their opinions out loud in the midst of the enemy. Why the hell hadn't anyone cautioned me to keep my mouth shut? If they'd explained the situation clearly to me, I might have listened to them.

"You'll be loved too, Mickey," Virginia added. My mother always disliked not being accepted as an equal. I hadn't ever heard her use the hateful words most of our family voiced in reference to Blacks in Chicago and Saint Louis. As for being loved, just not being hated would satisfy me.

. . .

After we passed through Provo, the location of Brigham Young University, most civilization was left behind. Forested mountains towered above us on our left and barren alkali desert fell away on our right. The sky was bright blue with hazy clouds, and the outside temperature hovered at one-hundred-degrees. We kept the dash vents open and the windows rolled down an inch to keep air circulating. A canvas bag filled with water hung over the front grill of the Pontiac to help cool the laboring engine.

Bounding jackrabbits, lonely ranches, and tiny towns at road intersections were the only relief across the desolate landscape.

Useless chatter dissipated and each of us burrowed into our own worlds. Al concentrated on maintaining a constant speed by shifting gears up and down as we climbed to higher elevations.

Virginia stared listlessly at the sparsely populated countryside passing by in a blur. She surely dreamed about a life of wealth, glamour, and sunny California beaches.

Peggy napped. She remained beautiful even when she slept. There wasn't any mouth hanging open, snoring, or careless drool from her. A tiny bead of perspiration showed at her hairline. That sweet droplet sparkled in the sunlight. She sleepily attempted to stretch out. I squeezed against my side of the car and willingly gave her all the room she wanted. The soles of her shoeless feet touched my leg. Electrified sensations surged through me. I wished I could lift her lovely feet onto my lap, but I didn't dare. Please forgive my sinful thoughts, Jesus.

I attempted to sleep. Eyes closed, I listened to the soft whine of the outside air flowing past the car. I heard the groans of the auto's chassis and the engine's surges of power on long uphill climbs. The tires thumped against the uneven asphalt. Restless human bodies shifted and breathing modulated. The car shuddered from bumper to bumper when we passed a semi-truck barreling along the highway in the opposite direction.

"Let's look for a nice place to stop and eat lunch," Virginia interrupted the reverie.

"Good idea," I piped up, trying to sound cheerful. "I'm hungry."

"There looks like a pleasant spot," Virginia pointed ahead of us.

"Yes it does," Al agreed, sounding grateful to hear her voice.

We pulled in a spotlessly-clean roadside rest area home to a weather-worn picnic table. As soon as we parked, everyone gratefully exited the car to stretch and walk about the lovely oasis we lucked upon. Al carried the cooler to the picnic table. Virginia spread a red and white-checkered tablecloth over the table and laid out our meal of homemade sandwiches wrapped in wax paper, a new bag of potato chips, a jar of sweet pickles, a half-gallon bottle of water, and Al's black and red-checkered thermos of coffee.

I attacked my food.

"These sandwiches are great," I said. "So are the potato chips and pickles."

"Thank you, Mickey," Virginia smiled.

"Yes, it's a good lunch," Al added. Once again, he'd missed an opportunity to be the first to offer her a compliment.

The sandwiches were delicious. I ate two luncheon meat and cheese with mustard sandwiches and all the chips I was allotted. Even though she was a couple of inches taller than me, Peggy was easily satisfied with one sandwich and a few chips.

She broke off and threw bits of her lunch to birds warily approaching us.

"These birds are pretty brave," she said. She didn't talk much on this trip and I felt terribly cheated by her silence. I loved the sound of her voice.

I watched the birds work up their courage to approach us more closely for fragments of food. A line of fearless ants began their determined march up the legs of the picnic table to retrieve and carry off any crumbs we might leave behind.

"There's a lizard!" I pointed to the base of a nearby cactus. Puffed up defiantly in the shade provided by the desert vegetation, the tiny creature swung its head in a sideways bob as it eyed us and stuck its tongue out as a warning. After having its say, it spun around raising a tiny sandstorm, and slithered away.

"I don't like lizards," Virginia complained.

"Me neither," Peggy added. "Especially after I found one in my bed."

"I remember that," Al said. "She lifted her covers and there sat a green monster. She let out such a scream."

"I was young then, Dad."

"I captured the frightened little thing and put it outside," Al laughingly joked.

"Quit teasing me about that silly incident, Dad," Peggy responded.

I hoped Peggy realized I wasn't afraid of lizards, and I was always ready to protect her from any and all dangers.

CHAPTER TWENTY

After good leg stretches, breathing lots of fresh air, and eating a pleasant lunch, we climbed back in the car. I felt better about being on the road and in the midst of our epic travel adventure to California. Virginia's tourist guide said the route we followed from Salt Lake City, Utah to Las Vegas, Nevada, crossed some of the most rugged and beautiful landscape in the western United States.

"This area of the American West is home to endless wonders of wind sculpted rocks spread across a vast wilderness," Virginia read from her tourist guide as if she was a movie actress delivering her lines. She added, "I love driving through this country. I told you a trip to California would be fun, Al."

"You were right, Virginia," Al replied meekly.

"I think it's pretty boring," Peggy said.

"When we get there, you'll love California, Peggy. You'll love the ocean and the beaches," Virginia said as she turned and smiled at the two of us in the back seat.

"I saw the ocean when I went to Florida," I bragged.

"Florida is beautiful too," Virginia replied wistfully. She

looked like she remembered happier times from her vagabond life of traveling after she'd freed herself from the burden of her five sons.

Her mood was improving, but I was sure she didn't want Al to think he in any way contributed. She loathed him, but really liked his daughter. And, she showered lots of love and affection on Peggy. That was fine with me. I didn't want to be responsible for filling the bottomless pit of the need for love that dominated her life.

We stopped in Cedar City, Utah for the night and rented a room in the cheapest motel. The room was crowded with one double bed and a rollaway. Damn. I'd have to sleep in the backseat of the car.

"Cedar City is a prosperous tourist city of seven thousand people who are surrounded by red rock outcroppings only hinting at the spectacular beauty of nearby Cedar Breaks National Monument, Bryce Canyon National Park and Zion National Park," Virginia read from her tourist guide. She liked to demonstrate that despite her limited sixth-grade education, she could read well.

As night fell, we walked the town's charming and tidy main street. I salivated over the smells escaping from a crowded café. Customers inside sat in large booths and ate steaks, roast beef, cheeseburgers, and eggs and bacon and fried potatoes with onions. Breakfast was served all day, the sign in the window declared.

We bought fresh lunchmeat and sliced American cheese at the local market. We walked back to the motel and finished off the loaf of bread we started our trip with. I wolfed down two sandwiches. We ate the last of the apples we brought with us.

It was dark when I walked out to the car for a dreaded night of cramped sleep in the uncomfortable back seat. At least I had the nightly symphony of insects to serenade me to sleep. It sounded like there were billions of them yelling at each other.

A bright, rising sun forced me awake. I slept better than expected for being stuck in the hard, ill-shaped, back seat of the Pontiac. I crawled out of the vehicle and unfolded and stretched my stiff body. After having my turn in the motel room bathroom, I was ready for the latest fun our vacation offered.

On this morning, we were greeted by a blue sky filled with towering stacks of billowy clouds and a quickening warm breeze. Al and I walked to the town market as Cedar City was just coming to life. I really enjoyed the awakening to a new day atmosphere in this small western town. Bird songs and clean, desert smells filled the air.

At the store, we bought a cellophane package of cinnamon rolls, and a refill of coffee for Al's thermos. Individual cups of coffee were too costly. Back in our tiny motel room, I ate three cinnamon rolls. I was still hungry and looked forward to lunch. Virginia liked to say I had a hollow leg. Al didn't say anything about how much I ate. He didn't want to offend either my mother or me. Peggy remained indifferent.

We left Cedar City behind and drove on through Utah. The sky clouded darkly, and sudden fierce thunderstorms and heavy rain lashed us. The storms passed and the sun broke through for a brief respite. Brilliant rainbows magically appeared. Quickly, more dark clouds filled the sky, and another spectacular display of heavy rain, sky-to-earth bolts of lightning, and eardrum-shattering, rolling thunder engulfed us.

When the storms paused in their relentless march, we pulled in rest stops or scenic pullouts to admire the fantastic reddish-colored hills and rock formations that led up to the surrounding mountains. The smell of the newly moistened desert vegetation and sandy soil was a sensory overload, a scent impossible to duplicate and bottle.

On our way to visit Zion National Park, we skirted the edge of Zion National Monument.

As we entered the park, Virginia read from her travel guide. "These towering monoliths are colored from deep blood-red to newly fallen snow-white. Mother Nature has generously endowed Southern Utah with great beauty. Castles, spires, bridges and storybook fairies were carved over thousands of years from multicolored rock. Whatever shapes the mind wants to see, even bears and other wild animals, exist here. Monsters scary enough to populate any child's nightmares can be imagined. There are no inhibitions to the fantasies filling every angle of nature's sculpturing." She smiled proudly after her excellent recitation.

These rock formations wouldn't be a big scare in my dreams. Cruel adults, brutal bullies, and abandonment ran roughshod through my nightmares. Being totally alone and helpless in a dark, merciless world dripping with evil was my all too frequent nightmare.

Back on Highway 91, we drove through the remote northwestern corner of Arizona, crossed into Nevada, and entered the small desert town of Mesquite. After being a prisoner to Naomi and enduring mind-numbing isolation for four years, I struggled to understand why people willingly imprisoned themselves in this terribly boring, nothingness of a desert.

Forty miles further on, we made a side trip south on State Road 12 and passed through the Valley of Fire, which looked as if a gigantic blaze burned in this remote place for thousands of years, and left behind many shattered and charred rock formations. This wasteland looked somewhat like the moonscape Buck Rogers landed on in the matinee movies, only the desolation was far more realistic and much more intimidating.

We ate lunch at a rest area on the northernmost shore of unimaginably transparent-blue Lake Mead. I hadn't ever seen so clearly and deeply in a body of water. We enjoyed the warm afternoon as we picnicked along the spotlessly-clean, pebbly shoreline. A gentle breeze barely roiled the surface of the lake.

"This is such a wonderful place," Virginia exulted.

We all nodded agreement. After our peaceful meal, we retraced our route back to Highway 91 and headed west again.

At dusk, we left the barren, alkali desert behind and descended to glittery Las Vegas, the gambling mecca home to thirty-thousand people. Route 91 turned to Main Street, which intersected with Fremont Street. The numerous brightly-lit casinos dazzled my eyes. Traffic crept along bumper to bumper, and smiling, carefree pedestrians crowded the wide sidewalks. Pulsing, multi-colored signs bragged Dean Martin and Jerry Lewis performed at the Sands, Joe E Lewis headlined at the El Rancho, Gloria De Haven starred at the Vegas, and Patti Page entertained at the Desert Inn.

We parked the car and joined other excited tourists on this balmy, desert evening. Signs clearly stated no one under eighteen was allowed on the gaming floors. Peggy and I stood outside on the sidewalk under the cascading lights of the Flamingo Hotel and Casino, as Al and Virginia tried their luck with penny slot machines.

The bright lights and non-stop activity were a vivid contrast to the wilds of nature we recently journeyed through.

People fervently praying for a payoff poured their money in the slot machines. Al and Virginia gambled alongside dozens of other hopefuls. They pulled handles. They won some. The winning and the clanging of their reward of pennies brought rare smiles to their faces. They pulled handles. They lost. Their faces returned to masks of disappointment. Finally, they gave a last shrug of defeat. They lost their five-dollars worth of pennies and the dream of a life-changing jackpot. It was another losing effort in the pursuit of nirvana.

"I thought for sure my machine was going to pay off," Virginia lamented. "Just one more pull of the lever and I might have won the jackpot."

"Maybe you should've kept trying," I said.

"I thought my machine was getting close," Al added.

"Maybe that's why they call them one-armed bandits," Peggy explained.

The mood was definitely deflated as we spent the night at a cheap motel on the outskirts of the city. Once again, the room was painfully small and I spent another night sleeping in the cramped back seat of the car.

I was awakened by the brightness and heat of the morning sun. Stiff and sweat stained, I clumsily climbed out of the Pontiac. I stretched my way to the motel room and waited for my turn to use the bathroom.

My consolation for a bad night's sleep was a real breakfast at a real café. We all ordered pancakes, which was the cheapest item on the menu. Al and Virginia drank cups of fresh, hot coffee. Peggy and I each had a glass of cold milk. I stared at and smelled the wonderful ham and eggs with fried potatoes and buttered toast people around us wolfed down. Oh well.

Pancakes beat cinnamon rolls. I piled on lots of butter and syrup. If we'd won a jackpot, we'd be eating steak and eggs.

We returned to our journey. We turned south to view and drive across massive Hoover Dam, the man-made marvel of poured concrete. Al parked the Pontiac and we walked on the dam. I gazed down from the dizzying height to the water far below. I imagined hundreds of men laboring under the blazing sun and dealing with extraordinary construction dangers. A sign said more than one-hundred workers died on the job.

We left Hoover Dam behind and made our way back to Las Vegas and turned southwest for the two-hundred-ninety-mile drive to Los Angeles. I already smelled the salty Pacific Ocean. I saw palm trees swaying in warm ocean breezes. I gawked at beautiful and glamorous movie stars.

A thick layer of boredom and silence descended upon the interior of the Pontiac as we traveled south across the desolate California desert. The sky turned hazy and it was too hot inside the car. I gasped for breath. Taking a break from the monotony of the drive, we stopped to take photos in front of a Joshua tree. While we posed next to the giant cactus, I once again appreciated the clean air and sweet smell of unpopulated wilderness.

Back on the highway, I wondered about the lives of laborers who worked under the merciless, hot sun to put up the endless miles of now sagging barbed-wire fencing. I also wondered why people used the road signs for target practice, when it would be just as easy and certainly more challenging, to set up a discarded tin can or soda bottle on top of a fence post and blast away.

CHAPTER TWENTY-ONE

As we neared Los Angeles, miles of orange groves surrounded us. It was a strange sight to see thousands of full-sized oranges hanging from endless rows of green-leafed trees. I never imagined oranges grew that way. I thought a person should be allowed to stop and pick this delicious fruit growing so close to the busy highway, but prominent signs warned about severe penalties for trespassing. A couple of those signs were riddled with bullet holes.

The traffic, the billboards, the buildings, and the smog grew denser as we relentlessly drove on to reach our magical vacation destination. It didn't appear a view of the Pacific Ocean would ever be possible and Virginia finally abandoned her silence.

"We'll see the coast soon. We'll see palm trees too," she sighed hopefully. "I love being close to the ocean and walking on the beach."

Peggy sat up straighter and looked out her window. I was torn between wanting to spy on her every physical and emotional reaction to the approaching wonderland of glamorous movie stars and sunny, blissful beaches, and my own need to watch the rapidly changing sights from my window.

Many years ago, my brothers and I huddled on the walkway of a forty-foot-high, rust-flaked, storage tank in foul-smelling Chicago. We looked to the west and visualized Dad and Baby John frolicking in the surf, and building sand castles on one of California's perfectly clean, spacious beaches.

Ben bragged he'd find Dad and Baby John some day.

"Dad's such an asshole," Tommy stated. I remembered Tommy's anger when Dad abandoned our family and took Baby John with him to California. Dad left my oldest brother, Tommy, behind in Chicago, and Tommy hated Dad for that slight.

I shifted back to the reality of the moment. It was growing dark as we navigated our way through the traffic-clogged city that appeared endless.

"Turn right here, Al," Virginia instructed impatiently as she struggled to follow her map.

We were lost and desperate. We decided to take a chance on a two-story, pink-stucco hotel next to Angels Flight, a tourist attraction Virginia read about in her travel guide.

After squeezing in a parking place on the street, we gathered our overnight essentials and walked to our possible refuge.

The Angels Flight cars progressed noisily up and down their tracks and looked like a part of the fun vacation I anticipated.

"We can take a ride on those cars tomorrow," Virginia said. She then directed accusingly at Al, "I know at least that'll be exciting."

The accommodations offered to us at the hotel contained only one double bed.

"No rollaway beds are available," the unfriendly clerk stated. "This is the only room we have available. Are you going to take it?"

Virginia reluctantly signed the registry and paid the exorbitant room charge.

The hotel reeked of mildew and age and resembled what I thought a skid row flophouse must be like. Foul-smelling hallways branched out from the shabby lobby. I wondered if behind most of the numbered doors, hard-drinking transients were downing bottles of cheap rotgut. As we searched along the dim hallways for our room, the hotel echoed with angry drunken arguments, and vibrated from doors being slammed shut.

"This is terrible, Al," she said when we entered our dingy, depressing room.

"Shall we try somewhere else, Virginia?" He looked and sounded disconsolate. He'd failed her again.

"No. We're stuck here for tonight. If you hadn't gotten us lost, we'd have done much better."

"I'm sorry, Virginia."

She looked the room and bedding over. She shook her head from side to side with disgust.

"This rotten place is where we have to sleep tonight." She directed her statement at Al as if he was the most incompetent person who ever walked the face of the earth.

Total exhaustion made this moldy cave bearable. Actually, in Los Angeles, this sort of seedy accommodation was the best we could afford. Al and I went in search of a nearby market to buy a loaf of bread, luncheon meat and cheese. Virginia and Peggy waited behind with the room door locked, and a chair propped against the door knob.

. . .

We decided the neighborhood was too dangerous for me to spend the night in the car, so Peggy and I'd sleep on the floor and share a blanket. She was fourteen. I was thirteen.

She wore soft-cotton, panda-bear decorated pajamas. I wore white jockey undershorts and a tee shirt.

"Good night, you two," Virginia said from the bed she reluctantly shared with Al Davey. She turned the table lamp out. I welcomed the semi-darkness. After a few deep inhalations in his lungs, and exhalations toward the ceiling, the red glow from the tip of Al's Pall Mall cigarette disappeared. He crushed his cherished last smoke of the day in the ashtray.

Peggy rolled onto her side with her back to me. I conceded most of the blanket and gave her as much space as I could.

She easily went to sleep. I lay uncomfortable and tense under my small portion of the covers. The room grew quieter and colder. I tugged to get a tiny bit more of my share of the blanket.

As I huddled in a fetal position, a draft of cold air washed over me.

I crawled further under the covers next to Peggy.

Her breathing was like the softest sigh of a breeze I ever heard. I was intoxicated by the sweet smell of her body. I tried to force myself to sleep, but her body heat radiated over me and her soft presence engulfed me. Suddenly, she curled in a fetal position. She pushed her buttocks against the front of me. Our bodies were touching in a terrifying way.

Please be merciful to me, God.

My curse was not merciful. It arose to a point beyond what I ever experienced before.

Even if the torture of having to lie next to my lovely stepsister did cause me to die, I wanted it to go on and on. I wanted the pain to go on forever. The next moment, I prayed this night would end as quickly and painlessly as possible.

Like a contented housecat, Peggy straightened and stretched her body to its full length. She rolled onto her stomach with her face turned to me. Her warm breath cascaded over me. I reluctantly turned my face away from her. I stared up at the dark-shadowed ceiling.

I prayed again, "Please let bright daylight flood this room, Jesus. Save me from my unbearable torture, Lord."

She turned back onto her side. Her bottom pressed against me again.

Was she was dreaming of her handsome Prince Charming? Was he holding her tightly in his muscular arms and pressing himself against her firm body? Did he offer her tender kisses on her soft lips? From head to toe, I was on fire. A scorching fever throbbed in my skull. Can the blood of a human bubble up to a boil and overflow out through their eyeballs?

Al and Virginia shifted in their sleep. His snores became louder. I rolled out from under the covers. I desperately needed to cool off. Quickly, I was too cold. I wondered if dying felt exactly like the distress I now suffered.

Too fearful of being discovered to masturbate, there wasn't any relief or escape for me on this wondrous, but horribly frustrating night.

Peggy awoke in the morning with a catlike stretch and sensuous yawn. She paused as if she was deep in thought. She turned and stared into my eyes. Suspicion clouded her face. Her gaze penetrated my soul. I saw a hint of the feverish night radiate from her suddenly blushing face. My blood flowed and my weary penis immediately swelled, but I concentrated on thoughts of nothingness to calm it down. She turned away from me. Did she now despise me more than she ever had before?

She scurried out of our rumpled bed and claimed the bathroom. When she reappeared dressed in pedal pushers and a blouse, I knew I'd disappeared from her thoughts. I was safe.

CHAPTER TWENTY-TWO

Although it was already becoming smoggy, an otherwise pleasant morning greeted Al and me as we walked to a nearby market. We bought a cellophane-wrapped package of cinnamon rolls, a quart bottle of cold milk and a thermos refill of coffee. Al always carried his thermos with him and refilled it at lunch counters and food shops. It appeared the most satisfying activities in his life were smoking Pall Mall cigarettes and drinking coffee from his black and red checkered thermos bottle.

"Is this what you call a continental breakfast, Al?" Virginia commented with disdain when we arrived back at our seedy motel room.

I tried to ignore her complaining. It was turning to a picture-perfect California day and I looked forward to being a tourist in sun-soaked Los Angeles.

After we'd finished our continental breakfast, we gratefully checked out of the stinking, fleabag hotel and carried our luggage to the car. With everyone feeling more hopeful, we walked to the Angels Flight railroad.

. . .

Angels Flight operated as a funicular railroad. Two separate cars attached to each other by a single cable, traveled up and down a three-hundred-foot slope. The railroad connected the street at the bottom of the steep hill, to another street at the top. The orange and black cars traveled on a single track until they reached the middle of the incline and there the single track separated to two tracks, allowing the cars to pass side by side. We rode to the top and after a short wait, back to the bottom. The railroad was noisy and rough and passed my test as a fun amusement park ride.

We couldn't afford to visit Disneyland, which recently opened to great fanfare, or famous Knott's Berry Farm. We drove to the free public beach Virginia located in her cherished travel guide. With a loaf of bread, a package of bologna, a package of sliced cheese, a jar of mustard, a bag of potato chips, and a large bottle of Coca Cola, we enjoyed a modest picnic on the sandy beach.

On this warm, sunny California day, Virginia, Peggy, and I rolled up our pant legs and played in the surf gently tumbling up on the beach. Al sat on a towel and smoked. Finally, he couldn't resist, and joined us. Our playtime in the Pacific Ocean temporarily halted Virginia's unending criticism of him, and constant complaints about what a lousy vacation he provided.

The next day, an event took place that I had imagined, hoped for, and dreaded. We'd meet my brothers, Ben and John, at the beach. I hadn't seen Ben for four and a half years. I hadn't seen John for eight and a half years. I was excited to see my brothers, but I also worried about how they'd react to me. This California setting was vastly different from when we were young, dirt-poor, and living in the industrial slums of North Chicago.

As we waited near the parking lot, I saw the expected car arrive and park. As the group of people exited the vehicle, Ben draped his arm around a pretty girl. A real, live, breathing human-female allowed my crude brother to embrace her. His girlfriend's mother provided the car ride that enabled this momentous, family reunion.

Our two groups merged. Ben showered overly-dramatic hugs onto Virginia, and my beloved stepsister, Peggy. He extended an overly-manly handshake to Al Davey.

"Hello, little brother," Ben bellowed as he approached me. He slapped me on my back with one hand. With his other hand, he grasped my hand in a dominating handshake.

Only fifteen months separated Ben and me in age, but he stood several inches taller than I and showed real muscle on his body. He sported a surfer tan, while I remained as pale as a ghost, and as scrawny as a scarecrow. He displayed a cocky smile and showed off his attractive girlfriend like he'd won the biggest prize at the carnival. He relaxed a bit when he realized I wasn't a threat to him in any way. He could make his usual blustery impression on the world without any concern for my existence.

My youngest brother, John, who was born a seven-month preemie, stood short in stature, even for a ten-year-old. Virginia hadn't seen her "Baby John" since our father abandoned our family eight and a half years before and took John with him to California. John acted uncomfortable and unsure about this reunion with his real mother. Virginia hugged him with great, motherly warmth and declared "I love you" again and again. Ben reported to Virginia that John viewed our father's second wife as his real mother. It was obvious Virginia's overwrought show of affection threw John's fragile world way off kilter.

John and I struggled to decide how to respond to each other. At least I was able to say, "Hello, little brother."

My world continued in its usual twisting chaos. I didn't have a clue how to react emotionally or physically to this bizarre happening. Except for this brief reunion, I knew I wasn't invited back as a member of Ben's, John's, or my supposed father's lives. I wasn't considered for full membership in that branch of the Shafer family. I was abandoned at the age of five by my supposed father, and sold in slavery at age nine by my mother. Those were both final moments of parental obligation to me. Any help beyond those ages, was strictly charity without any future guarantees.

I watched Ben show easy familiarity to his and my stepsister, Peggy. This was the Peggy I loved with all of my heart. This was the Peggy I'd lain next to, in agony, just the night before. Jealousy scorched through me like a wind-whipped prairie fire. Ben overflowed with confidence and dismissed me as irrelevant. It was the worst version of my older brother I remembered from our early years together on the streets of Chicago. Once again, I hated him as much as I could hate any human being.

The joyful reunion ended. Ben and John stayed behind in the wonderland of 1955 California. I desperately wanted to be part of their world and escape from the Mormons back in Ogden, Utah. The possibility of me rejoining my supposed family wasn't ever mentioned. Just as I did during my childhood in Chicago, I felt like a neighborhood waif who wandered through a stranger's front door, and was allowed to sit at their dinner table only out of pity. The nasty gossip and cruel jokes about me looking like the milkman weren't just ignorant humor. I truly was a blonde-haired, blue-eyed bastard without any family.

The next morning, we left Los Angeles for the long, bleak drive back to the land of Joseph Smith, Brigham Young, and their fervent flock. I'd been given an eight-day pass from a high-walled prison, and was now returning to finish serving out my life sentence. Not even the blazing sun we drove towards could burn the blackness out of me. Ahead lay Utah, the land ruled by my tormentors.

Except for being close to Peggy, it was a torturous drive back to Ogden. Virginia stayed in the foulest of moods. Al remained hopeless in his lack of understanding. The beauty of the desert we sped across was clouded by the bleak future awaiting each one of us.

CHAPTER TWENTY-THREE

A couple of months later, back in Ogden, an unexpected knock at the front door of the house startled Virginia. Her face lit up with apprehension. Nervously, she rushed to answer.

"Benny," she exclaimed.

She pulled my older brother in the house, shut the door, and hugged him warmly. A bedraggled and exhausted Ben returned her affection. He then gave our stepsister Peggy a big hug and Peggy returned his embrace enthusiastically. Goddamn her to hell. She wouldn't hug me at all. Ben gave Al a manly handshake.

Ben nodded half-heartedly in my direction. "Hello, little brother." The "brothers surviving on the streets together" comradeship from our childhood in Chicago was on life-support.

My mind was in turmoil. I envied and hated Ben's ability to embrace people with overwrought enthusiasm. I didn't know how to hug people with the fervor so many others easily displayed. I always feared the reaction I'd get. How did you know who you were supposed to hug and for how long? Hugs could signal danger. Virginia always gave me loving hugs when she abandoned me. Did Ben forget she left him at the orphanage in Saint Louis and put him up for adoption? I guess he ignored her betrayals and lived past that horrible reality. I always tried to push my abandonment pain deep inside. I hoped the pain would stay hidden, but the demon residing there always pushed the pain back up to my brain. I didn't think about Naomi much anymore, but her abuse left me with a mistrust of people I feared would last forever. Her screaming voice and hard fists lingered as a potent reminder of the foolishness of trusting any human, especially my mother.

And now Ben showed up in Ogden to reclaim his share of our mother's affection. He was welcome to both his and my meager amount. I didn't rely on any affection from her.

One of Ben's constant fights with our bully father, Orin, was worse than usual. Of course, for me, it was always my "supposed father."

"I told Dad I didn't want to live with him anymore," Ben stubbornly declared.

"Well, leave then," Orin replied. "I don't give a shit what you do, Ben."

Ben packed his suitcase and hitchhiked from Los Angeles to Ogden. A lanky, physically attractive, fifteen-year-old boy with dark wavy hair and pale blue eyes, he traveled the highways alone. I wondered if my older brother would tell me about the kind of men who gave him rides. He and I shared many experiences with sexual predators on the streets of Chicago when we were young. I was sure there were many of those sickos out on the open road looking for vulnerable and desperate youths like Ben.

. . .

Ben and I slowly reconnected as brothers. He brought me up to date on events that took place during the four years I was trapped with the abusive Naomi.

After Virginia consigned me to my hellish life with the monster Naomi, she, with Ben in tow, the last of her five sons she was in possession of, hitchhiked to Saint Louis, Missouri. Once again, she sought refuge at her mother Goldie's crowded apartment.

It didn't take long until she found a man who didn't want kids around. Her new man wanted her to travel to Florida with him for sun and fun. Our mother took Ben to a Christian Church orphanage in Saint Louis and convinced them she couldn't care for her ten-year-old son anymore.

Ben arrived at the orphanage with one change of clothes and a few personal possessions. He carried his favorite picture of Jesus Christ showing Jesus with a bared and bleeding heart. He pinned his treasure to the wall at the head of his narrow dormitory cot.

"You can't display Catholic heresy here," an angry matron told him.

"That's my favorite picture, ma'am."

"This is a Christian Orphanage, Benny. While you're here, you'll be a Christian."

"My daddy was a Catholic. He'll be mad at me if I don't stay a Catholic."

"Your father abandoned you. He abandoned all of your family. Your father is an evil man."

"No he isn't. He told me he loves me."

"If your father or mother loved you, you wouldn't be in this orphanage, Benny. Your father and mother don't care one iota what happens to you. You better shut up and behave while you're here. Do you want to end up at the reform school where they beat kids with rubber hoses? That won't be any fun."

She ripped the picture of Jesus and his bleeding heart from the wall. She tore Ben's treasure in bits.

"If you want to go to heaven, you have to learn the right path to salvation, Benny. Catholics don't go to heaven."

"I don't want to be part of your religion. I want to stay Catholic."

"Don't talk back to me!"

SLAP!

OW!

"You better follow the rules here or you'll be in big trouble!"

People visited the orphanage to look over the orphans. Some of the healthiest and prettiest of the youngest children were taken in homes for trial periods, and if they passed the test, might be adopted. Foolish Ben thought some kind couple would choose him as their child to adopt. It didn't happen. A rough looking, ten-year-old street boy like him was out of luck.

Ben prayed to God every day. He prayed and waited for Mom to come back and rescue him. He wanted to be free from all the orphanage's endless rules. He didn't like to be disciplined.

When the local community held a parade, the orphans marched as a group. They wore their orphanage uniforms and marched in time to the music of a local high school band. They hoped some kind soul who watched them marching by would welcome them in their home as a foster child, and maybe adopt them. Ben marched and smiled his best.

Ben was a healthy, sturdy boy. Soon, he found a foster home on a farm. The couple, whose son was serving in the U. S. Army in Korea, needed a boy for labor. Ben grew to view this elderly couple as Grandpa and Grandma. They weren't terribly mean, but hard work was a normal part of their daily life. They expected Ben to work just as hard as their own son worked before he went off to Korea to fight the commies.

Ben didn't like farm work. He wanted time to play. On a farm, chores never ended. A city boy, Ben longed for the freedom of the streets of Chicago. Hustling and stealing were essential for survival on those streets. Running free on city streets was much more fun than the drudgery of farm life.

One day, after a few months on the farm, angry at being reprimanded by Grandma Farmer, Ben hid under the front porch. He was thinking about Mom and hating her for not showing up to save him. He felt the whole world was against him. He didn't like sitting on the musty earth under the porch. Spider webs alive with black widows surrounded him. He heard rats moving about in the dark corners.

"You come out of there, Ben," Grandma Farmer yelled when she discovered where he was hiding.

"No!"

"I said come out right now."

"Hell no, I won't come out."

"Don't use that kind of language, Ben. Good Christians don't talk like that. You want to go to hell?"

"I won't go to hell. I'm a good Catholic."

"There's no such thing as a good Catholic." Grandma Farmer stomped a foot on the porch.

"Don't say anything bad about being Catholic." Now, he shed real tears.

"Who do you think you are, Ben? Your own Mother put you up for adoption."

"That's a Goddamn lie. She wouldn't ever do that."

"I told you I don't want to hear that kind of language. Your mother did put you up for adoption. Get off of your high horse, Ben. Nobody will adopt a kid like you."

"All that stuff's a big lie." Covered with dirt and face streaked from tears, he crawled out from underneath the porch. "My mother wouldn't ever put me up for adoption," he assured himself as he looked down at his beat-up, dirty shoes.

Grandma Farmer glared down at him.

"Send me back to the orphanage, Grandma. I don't want to live here anymore."

"Oh, don't you worry, Ben. You're going back to the orphanage. We'll see how you like that."

Sent back to the orphanage, eleven-year-old Ben found out Virginia did make him available for adoption. Grandma Farmer told the truth. His own mother abandoned him and she'd allow strangers to adopt and keep him forever. So many awful things could happen to him. He might never see Mom again.

A man who said he was an airline pilot befriended Ben during a visit to the Orphanage. The man became a sort of weekend foster parent. Ben told this man his mother put him up for adoption and he didn't want to live with strangers. He bragged how he planned to run away and make his way in the world. The man didn't want Ben to end up on the streets and in ruin. He used his resources to track Virginia down and pressured her to rescue Ben.

Ben turned twelve-years-old on his trip from Saint Louis, Missouri to Waverly, Colorado aboard a train. Goddamn. My older brother took the same kind of train trip I took to be reunited with our Mother. We were both twelve-years-old when our torturous reunions took place.

I now knew part of Ben's story. But, there was more.

CHAPTER TWENTY-FOUR

B en lived with Virginia, Al Davey, and Peggy for a year or so in Waverly, Colorado, Cheyenne, Wyoming, and Ogden, Utah. Virginia saw an article in the Ogden newspaper about my oldest brother, Tommy. Now a soldier in the US Army and stationed in Germany, he won a commendation for his work at the base motor pool. Damn. Virginia found another of her abandoned sons. Without consulting Tommy, she contacted the army and told them he was only sixteen-years-old.

Because Tommy was underage, the army had to discharge him. That was a bad move on her part. Tommy really liked the Army, he was working in the motor pool, and was living off base with a German woman. After the Army flew him back to the USA for separation from the military, he showed up in Ogden, Utah, very angry at our mother, Virginia. He constantly caused trouble and made her and Ben's lives miserable. Once again, Ben was Tommy's punching bag.

"Come on, Ben. Let's spar. You need to learn how to box," Tommy said. He punched Ben really hard in the stomach and chest. Ben tried to box with Tommy, but he was hopelessly overmatched. Tommy laughed at Ben's frustration. Tommy never saw mercy in his life and he didn't show mercy for Ben or anyone else.

Tommy was sent to Boy's Town in Omaha, Nebraska, by a judge in Chicago with Virginia's approval, when he was twelve-years and two-months old. Abandonment and pain were the only realities on his rocky road to survival.

"Come on, Ben. You need to toughen up."

Tommy delivered a hard slap to Ben's face.

"That hurt, Tommy!"

Just like our father before he abandoned us, Tommy delivered a hard slap to the back of Ben's head.

"Quit hitting me, Tommy."

"Don't be a fucking baby, Ben. And don't ever touch any of my stuff. If you do, I'll break both your arms." Tommy grabbed Ben in an arm lock and threw him to the ground.

"Jesus, Tommy. You nearly broke my arm."

Al Davey ordered Tommy to move out of the house. Cast out again, Tommy disappeared and avoided any contact with his family.

My history lesson continued.

In the spring, a year before I left Chicago and rode a train to Ogden, Utah, my mother Virginia, harboring huge regrets over her marriage to Al Davey, suffered another attack of wanderlust. She left Al and Peggy and everything that wouldn't fit in her suitcase behind, and she and Ben hitchhiked to Los Angeles. After six days of living in a seedy motel and eating bologna sandwiches, she asked Ben if he'd like to visit his father for a weekend. Ben brightened up at the prospect of seeing his dad.

After telling him Dad would pick him up, Virginia left Ben standing on a street corner in busy downtown Los Angeles. Ben didn't have a clue what Dad looked like, or what kind of car he drove. Ben watched every approaching and passing vehicle with a man at the wheel. He hoped it would be his loving father. Many cars passed him. Some male drivers slowed down and looked him over. Ben recognized their intentions and looked away. The rejected predators drove on to search for more willing prey. Finally, a car pulled up to the curb where Ben waited.

The man at the wheel leaned out of the driver's window. "Are you Ben?"

"Yeah, I'm Ben."

"Get in, Ben. I'm Orin. Your mother said I'm your father."

Ben didn't comprehend the man's crude and cruel joke. He climbed in the front seat of the stranger's car. He sat next to the man who was supposed to be his father. As they drove south through the congested city, Ben marveled at his father's large, and seemingly luxurious, Hudson automobile.

"Do you remember me, Ben?"

"I sure do," Ben said with exaggerated enthusiasm.

"My wife's name is Pat," Orin said. "Your youngest brother, John, is eight-years-old. You probably don't remember him."

"I remember, John." Ben said. "He was just learning to walk the last time I saw him. That was back in Chicago when we were all together as a family."

"I want you to do me a favor, Ben," Orin said. "I want you to call Pat, "Mom.""

"Why?"

"That's what she likes."

"Sure," Ben said. "I'll call her mom."

. . .

Ben spent the weekend with "Dad" and his new family, who lived in a small house, with a small swimming pool in the small backyard. Ben was seduced by the lure of the sunny California lifestyle. Everything seemed large and wonderful. When Virginia called to arrange picking him up, he told her he didn't want to go back to living in the motel with her.

"I need you, Ben," she lamented.

"I want to live with my father," Ben pleaded. "I want to stay in Lawndale."

"Please don't abandon me, Ben."

"Please, Mom." Now, Ben was crying. "I love you Mom, but I want to stay here with my father, and my brother John."

"If that's what you want, Ben," Virginia replied with her most guilt-inducing tone. "I'll try to get by on my own."

From Hollywood, Virginia finally talked to Al Davey over the phone. Al cried and begged her to return to Ogden and give him another chance. Running out of money, she carefully calculated her needs for survival and minimal comfort. She left Ben with his father in California, and returned to Utah alone. Her pursuit of freedom from Al Davey was postponed.

Both physically and mentally, Ben survived our years apart much better than I. With Tommy absent from the scene, he showed lots of bluster. He even possessed a trace of athleticism and liked to demonstrate his advantage over me. He took a lot of abuse from our oldest brother and I guess he needed to pass it down to me. It was a bigger and older brother's obligation.

Totally self-absorbed, he could recognize my presence if he chose to. He could also simply forget I existed. If I disappeared, he owned my small share of our mother's attention. That was the battleground he chose for him and me. Which one of us did Mom love the most? He absolutely hated to think I was competition for the meager allowance of love Virginia allotted for her five sons. The truth was, I didn't want any of her affection, and didn't expect anything from her, other than a roof over my head.

During one of his runaway-from-Dad visits to Ogden, I made a serious mistake in my interaction with my older brother.

Ben and I were changing our clothes after a dirty, outdoor job. When I pulled my belt out of my trouser loops, I made a careless, ineffectual snap at him.

"Oh!" His eyes lit up. A big smile gripped his face. "You want to have a belt snapping fight, Mickey?"

Ben whipped his belt out of his trouser loops. Wielding a wider and longer belt than I did, his first snap was accurate and hard. His belt snap caught my forearm. I felt intense pain. I made a weak snap in response and missed. I wore a thin tee shirt and another hard, accurate snap from Ben hit my chest. I felt like I'd been burned with a blowtorch.

"This is fun," Ben exclaimed gleefully as he danced crazily around me. He'd gotten the rhythm of belt snapping.

"Come on, Mickey!"

Crack. His belt hit my arm.

Crack. His belt hit my stomach.

Each of his belt hits felt like strips of my skin were crudely cut with a knife, grabbed, and peeled away, leaving raw flesh exposed.

I made a desperate snap at him. It barely touched him.

"Oh. You got me, Mickey." He bounced about with increasing, demonic excitement. His face showed the glee of a cat pawing at a wounded and dying bird. His eyes widened and grew brighter. He put all his strength behind the snaps of his belt.

Crack.

Crack.

His body vibrated with frenzy. The joy he felt at inflicting painful wounds on my body glowed from his face.

In shock from the terrible pain, I quit snapping at him. I stood motionless. His eyes bulged with excitement. All of his long-suppressed jealousy and hatred for me erupted. I was born too soon after him and took his mommy away.

Crack.

Crack.

Burning pain layered upon burning pain. I made another futile snap at him. I missed. My resistance restored his fervor and inspired him to continue his merciless assault.

Crack.

Crack.

Suddenly he stopped. His belt dropped from his clenched hand. He looked bored. He eyed me with contempt.

"Had enough, Mickey?" he taunted. His laughter lost its sense of glee. His eyes lost their brightness.

I didn't say anything. I couldn't speak without sparking agonizing pain. I erased the look of contempt from his face, though. I moved closer to him and made another weak snap. My belt glanced harmlessly off his arm. Without much eagerness, but with deadly determination, he picked up and continued to snap his belt against my body. He wanted my total, unconditional surrender.

Crack.

Crack.

"Now you had enough, Mick?" He muttered breathlessly. "Do you give up?"

I stood motionless. I stayed silent. I couldn't lift my arms.

I'd die before I said, "I give up."

"Man," he gasped. "That was fun." It appeared his hatred was satiated. He lost the desire to punish me more.

Slowly and stiffly, I lifted my arms. I peeled off my sweat and blood-soaked tee shirt. Black, red and purple welts covered my stomach, chest, shoulders, and arms. Blood bubbled along the edges of my rapidly rising welts.

The smile disappeared from his face. The animalistic glee that twisted his features turned to horror. He rushed to the bathroom. I heard him vomit.

"Why didn't you say something?" he asked when he reappeared in the doorway wiping puke from his lips. "Look at yourself."

I couldn't put any words together. I did question myself. What should've I said? "I've had enough. I give up." There wasn't any way I'd ever say those words to him.

He cried. He blubbered. I walked in the bathroom. I saw myself in the mirror. Except for my face and neck there wasn't any undamaged skin visible. Now, I wanted to vomit.

"Why didn't you say something?" he cried out again. He wanted to place the fault of his brutality on me.

"There wasn't anything to say," I yelled.

"Please don't let Mom or anyone else see what I did," he pleaded. "Please don't."

"Fuck you!"

"I'll give you everything I own, Mickey. I'll give you everything."

"Go to hell." He wanted me to end his suffering immediately. Fuck him. Breathing caused my skin to erupt in flames. I knew I'd suffer for days.

I hid my wounds and my pain from everyone. Nobody ever discovered what took place in that room. I fantasized about ways to kill Ben. Nightly, I prayed to God for his death

CHAPTER TWENTY-FIVE

Ben and I shared some good times on his run-away-from-dad visits to Ogden, Utah. We rented tough trail horses at a riding stable in the foothills of the Wasatch Mountains. We rode along narrow, rocky paths those sure-footed equines wore in the mountainsides. Often, a rider needed to allow the horses their head so they could navigate the precarious footing. If you wanted to stay on top of the beasts, you had to let them know you weren't going to be rubbed out of the saddle against thick sagebrush, or pulled forward over their necks by a sudden head lowering. Those were two of the favorite tricks of these crafty, seasoned rental horses.

I conquered my nightmare of never being able to climb up onto a horse while everyone else galloped away in the distance and left me behind, lying on the ground, alone and helpless. I stayed aboard these wide barreled, oversized, trickster ponies and easily rode over the treacherous, nerve-wracking terrain.

. . .

Ben and I borrowed Al's bolt-action, twenty-two-caliber rifle. We hiked to a remote wilderness to camp and target shoot.

Ben climbed a tall, wide-branched tree to check out a large birds nest. "There are three eggs in this nest," he shouted down to me.

The angry red-tailed hawk came home. She screamed and made swooping lunges at him. I fired six quick shots at the irate bird, barely missing.

"Quit shooting, Mickey," Ben screamed during my volley. He rapidly descended the rough-barked tree.

He looked over his scraped hands. "Shit, Mickey. I felt and heard those bullets whizzing past me. They were really close. You could've killed me!"

"I wasn't going to hit you."

"You're crazy Mickey. You almost shot me."

"Hey. You didn't want the hawk to get you, did you?"

"You're a crazy fucker, Mickey."

I didn't understand why he was so upset. I was just playing out a western movie scene.

Feeling no need for a tent, we camped overnight under a sky filled with billions of pulsing stars. Shivering in a frigid morning, we cooked breakfast over our wood campfire, took naked dips in the fast-moving, ice-cold stream, and stretched out naked on the rocky shoreline, basking in the warming sunshine to thaw out our shivering bodies.

Ben seemed a bit cautious of me after the hawk incident. I was sure I didn't intend to kill him. I didn't mind. He now worried whether or not I was crazy enough to really shoot him.

. . .

Ben didn't have to contend with the serious hatred from the Mormons I faced every day. They excluded him from their society and from any decent jobs, but he accepted that. He had an escape available. Despite his tumultuous relationship with our asshole father, he missed the backyard pool and California lifestyle. In California he enjoyed equal rights, equal opportunities, and girlfriends. He bragged about the pretty girls a guy could meet in Los Angeles. He even met girls he liked when he went to church.

"It's a different world in California, Mickey," he boasted. "My best friend owns a hopped-up Chevrolet sedan with tuck and roll upholstery. There're lots of pretty girls to date. These Mormon girls won't even talk to me. Nobody in California cares what your damn religion is. There are good jobs to be had. You can't get a good job in Ogden unless you're a Mormon. I hate Utah."

Ben decided to make another attempt to live with his California family. Maybe, the constant cruelty of our father would magically disappear. Maybe, Dad wouldn't criticize him all the time. Ben threatened to thumb his way back to the coast. A worried Virginia and concerned Al Davey came up with money for a train ticket. For some reason, Virginia showed motherly concern over Ben hitchhiking alone on dangerous highways.

Ben returned to live his life with our father and youngest brother, John. California remained a magical wonderland in my mind. I stayed a forgotten and never considered outsider to my supposed father's and brother's world. If only they'd embrace and welcome me, I could escape my hopeless existence among the Joseph Smith worshippers.

I told myself Mormon oppression was still a better world than my brutal bondage to Naomi. I was free to move about. I needed to remember I was a despised pariah. I needed to recognize and avoid the religion-inspired enemies lurking every-where in Utah.

I reluctantly left my warm bed on Christmas morning, 1955. In the living room stood a modest tree adorned with Virginia's best decorations. Under the tree were a good number of presents, most with Virginia's name on them. Al sat on the edge of the couch, his face filled with great anticipation. He nervously puffed a Pall Mall as he waited for Virginia to open the gifts he'd so thoughtfully and generously bought for her.

"Merry Christmas, Virginia," he said confidently.

He watched her face closely as she struggled to decide which gift to remove his clumsy wrappings from first. He waited for her wonderful words of praise for his excellent choices. He envisioned her smiles, hugs and kisses.

She removed the colorful Christmas wrapping from a new roasting pan.

She removed the colorful Christmas wrapping from a new coffee pot.

She ripped away the colorful Christmas wrapping from a new waffle iron.

She angrily ripped away the ribbon Al clumsily scotch taped to a new vacuum cleaner.

"These are all perfect purchases for a hired housekeeper, Al," she said bitterly. She turned and gave him a withering glare of contempt. "They aren't gifts for a wife. Gifts are something personal. Like a bottle of perfume, or a silk neck scarf."

He winced at her words. His hands shook nervously. A towering, black cloud descended on Christmas morning.

"I thought you'd be happy, Virginia." He looked absolutely crushed. He was totally clueless. The thought of buying her a bottle of her favorite cologne and a pretty scarf never entered his unromantic mind.

Peggy smiled as she opened her gifts of clothing. She wouldn't show us the new undergarments Virginia bought for her. She seemed especially pleased with those. Once again, I was left to wildly imagine her naked body. Even seeing her walking around the house in her new undergarments would have fulfilled my earthly dreams, and prepared me for eternity in either heaven or hell.

My gift of a secondhand, red and white Schwinn bicycle satisfied me. I was grateful it was a boy's model and had new whitewall tires. I hoped I wouldn't encounter the original owner as I happily pedaled along the streets of Ogden, Utah.

Virginia stayed in her furious, black mood. I knew despite her total animosity towards Al, she'd still cook an excellent holiday meal. As she worked in the kitchen and used her new roasting pan, he groveled constantly, but to no avail. She remained ice-cold.

"This is a wonderful meal, Virginia," he praised after we took our places at the table.

She ignored him unmercifully and maintained her expression of absolute disgust with him and his ignorance. Her complete disappointment with Al, and their life together, was chillingly clear.

I enjoyed the delicious baked ham glazed with brown sugar, sweet potatoes dripping with butter and a big slice of pumpkin pie I'd covered with a generous amount of whipped cream. I did my best to ignore the tension between the warring couple.

Despite the odds against me, I survived to celebrate my fourteenth birthday.

"Hey, Mickey," Al said. "I've got some errands to do. Would you like to come along?"

"Sure, Al."

I didn't have any work for pay lined up on my momentous birthday. I hoped Virginia would remain restrained in her celebration. I didn't want to be completely forgotten, but I also didn't want attention focused on me.

Al and I spent an hour wandering around Montgomery Ward hardware and sporting goods departments. Next, we stopped at Al's favorite cafe for a cup of coffee. He even bought me a slice of apple pie with ice cream. I was always ready to eat. Al's frequent, uncharacteristic glances at his wristwatch raised my suspicions. Suddenly, he decided it was time to rush home.

When I walked in the house, I saw multi-colored ribbons and balloons hanging from the ceiling. A large square birthday cake and pitcher of red Kool-Aid sat in the center of the kitchen table. Flower-decorated paper plates, green plastic glasses, and neatly folded party napkins on the table completed the festive scene.

Virginia and Peggy greeted me with forced smiles. They couldn't hide the looks of distress on their faces.

"Surprise," they choked out. "Happy birthday, Mickey!"

For several marvelous moments, Peggy looked in my eyes. She was aware of my existence. She participated in an event honoring me. Gratitude and hope overwhelmed me.

"Thanks," I mumbled.

"Everybody's late for the party," Virginia apologized as she forced one of her motherly hugs on me. "I got the addresses of your home room classmates from school and sent all of them invitations. They should be here any minute."

Merciless God! Nobody from my home room class would attend a party for me, unless it was my funeral party. My mother was totally clueless about the reality of my life. She had no idea of the hell she'd brought down on me by staging her incredibly stupid party. Because of her ignorance, I faced even more dreadful harassment at school.

A knock at the front door restored Virginia's happy smile. She rushed to greet the first of my many guests. Standing on the front porch and sheepishly holding a wrapped gift was one of the prettiest girls from my class. She handed my present to Virginia. "I'm sorry," she said. "I can't stay for the party."

The pretty girl and I made momentary eye contact. It was obvious she saw no one from our school showed up to attend my stupid birthday party. Her expression reminded me of a soft-hearted person who couldn't stand the sight of a tiny mouse struggling to escape from a jubilant cat. I didn't need her pity. I didn't want her pity.

"Happy Birthday," she voiced quietly as she turned and hurried away.

Two kids I knew from the Salvation Army showed up for the big celebration of the fourteen years I spent staggering through my topsy-turvy life. We made a party of it. I got gifts. For a few minutes, I didn't think about the horrors awaiting me back among my classmates.

"Hey, freak! How was the big party, you retard!"

"You expected people to come to your stupid fucking party. You're such an asshole!"

"Shut up," the pretty girl who dropped off the present said, "Leave him alone."

Her words didn't slow down the barrage of harassment, but her sympathy gave me a momentary glimpse of humanity among these children.

"Don't ever send me such a stupid invitation again or I'll smash your face."

"You stupid fuck. I should kick the shit out of you."

I remembered a Bible quote: "But I say unto you, Love your enemies, bless them that curse you, do good to them that hate you, and pray for them which despitefully use you, and persecute you. St. Matthew 5:44"

I hated my enemies. I wanted them to die. I desperately wanted to have the power to kill each and every one of them with my own hands.

I did like the pretty girl who tried to help me. She didn't enjoy the torment unleashed on me, nor despised me. I liked her for more than her kindness though. I liked her silky brown hair, soft eyes, and constant smile which revealed perfectly-even, sparkly-white teeth. She was healthy. Her smooth skin glowed. She was beautiful. I could love her from afar. I could love her in secret. Neither she, nor anyone else, would ever know I loved her.

CHAPTER TWENTY-SIX

I woke to a clear and cold Sunday morning. Snow had fallen overnight.

During breakfast, Al commented, "With the new snowfall, this would be a perfect day to track and shoot deer."

"You know we have to go to church," Virginia reminded him impatiently.

"After church, maybe," he said. I knew there wasn't any maybe in his intentions.

We rushed Virginia and Peggy through their morning rituals as politely as possible. I felt the usual surge of excitement at the prospect of the upcoming hunt. Our time at the Salvation Army church services passed far too slowly. This year, I had a deer license with one tag, and I'd carry a borrowed .30-30 lever-action carbine. I loved the look and feel that the rifle made famous in cowboy movies. I could actually shoot at, and maybe kill a deer.

. . .

We arrived home after worshipping. Al and I quickly changed to hunting clothes, loaded our rifles and lunch in the trunk of the car, and backed out the driveway.

We drove to Ogden Canyon and parked just off the road below Al's favorite hunting area. By one o'clock in the afternoon we were hiking up a ridge overlooking a narrow gorge. We reached the top of the hill. I breathed deeply of the crystal-clear air and gazed at the natural wonderland of tall trees and sculptured stone surrounding us. We sat on a couple of chair size rocks and ate our sandwiches.

After we'd eaten and shared a cup of coffee from Al's thermos, we sat silent. I listened to birds calling and singing. A bee buzzed close to me. A nearby stream gurgled, producing a sound that seemed to be a clear expression of happiness. A whisper of wind sighed through the trees. Our relaxed breathing and rustle of our clothing became a part of the restrained symphony. I'd blended in and become a fixture in one of Earth's most magical places. Like one of the nearby boulders, undisturbed for thousands and thousands of years, I was a part of nature.

"Let's try another area," Al said as he suddenly stood. We quickly walked down the ridge on the other side of the gorge and reached the car.

After driving several miles over rough gravel road, we parked. We hiked a more gradual incline covered with dense, waist-high sagebrush. The going was tough, but the sagebrush smells were intoxicating, the sky brilliant blue, and the sun radiantly warming. I imagined we two were the only living humans on the earth.

We hiked two and a half miles uphill from the road when Al motioned me to silence. I breathlessly froze in my tracks. I heard the clicking-off of his rifle's safety. I watched him raise his thirty-aught-six. He carefully aimed. The blast from his shot thundered and the recoil forced him to flinch. My ears throbbed from the concussion.

He lowered his gun slightly. "I got him," he said. There was real excitement in his usually calm voice.

I hadn't seen his target. We scrambled down a fifteen-foot-deep crevice. We climbed back up to where the deer fell, twenty-five-yards distance from where Al fired. We'd been right on top of the huge buck. The creature's legs still thrashed in its death throes.

"Be careful," Al said. He raised his rifle and took aim at the heavily antlered head, but there wasn't any need for a second bullet. A final tremor surged through the deer's muscular body. His legs stiffened. His eyes glazed over. He lay motionless. He was dead.

"God. He must weigh over 200 pounds," Al said.

The buck was not only large in body; he showed a luxurious layer of fat and displayed a twelve-point spread of antlers. Inside me, the thrill over such a magnificent trophy was in furious battle with the horror I felt over the death we inflicted. A beautiful animal, he'd been in the prime of his life. A single bullet ended it. My only relief from the guilt I felt was the knowledge we were meat hunters.

Al went to work. He cut the throat to bleed the deer.

The testicles were large and swollen. "He was looking for a doe," Al said as he grabbed them with one hand. He sliced them off cleanly and threw them in the brush.

"Holy Jesus," I thought.

"Virginia won't cook them," he explained with a wicked grin.

He made a long incision along the abdomen. Steam from the warm body rose in the cold air.

"We're going to need lots of snow, Mickey. Scoop up all you can."

I scurried about gathering snow from nearby shaded areas. Al proceeded with the messy job of gutting the deer. He carefully removed the bladder and bowel and their contents to avoid contamination of the meat.

Al used the snow I piled near him to cleanse the inside of the deer. He cleaned and set aside the liver and what was left of the heart. His bullet was right on the mark. More than half of the heart was shattered in tiny fragments. After the cavity was thoroughly scoured, he put the heart and the liver back inside the deer and we packed it with snow.

"We need to take the rifles to the car first, Mick." He clapped his nearly frozen hands together. "I'm not sure how we'll manage to move this deer that far."

The adrenaline rush I felt over our hunting success made the downhill hike to the car pass quickly. We locked the rifles in the trunk and headed back to the deer, carrying the only helpful item we found, a coil of thick hemp-rope. The return hike uphill and tasks ahead were daunting. Neither of us talked. We needed to move rapidly and conserve our energy. As I trudged, I felt a bit deflated. I worried our prize would unexplainably disappear and we wouldn't ever be able to prove what a large mule deer Al shot. Locating and seeing the dead buck exactly where we left him restored my level of excitement.

Al cut slits between the tendons and bones of all four legs. He tied a loop of rope through both the back and front slits. We stepped in the loops, Al on the front legs, me on the back. We both leaned in our crude harness. With all of our strength, we pulled.

After a few hundred yards of effort, we realized it would be impossible to drag the heavy carcass with both of us side by side. The sagebrush grew too high and dense. The wide body of the buck continually snagged.

"We have to split this thing in two pieces," Al sighed with resignation.

We undertook the arduous task of sawing the deer in half with his hunting knife.

It took a while, with both of us taking turns, to finish. I was grateful when I finally stood up and stretched my aching body. We set off again, with Al dragging the front half and me dragging the rear. Daylight was fading too rapidly.

Al's desire to keep the head of the buck proved impossible. The antlers constantly tangled in the thick sagebrush. He used his hunting knife to saw the head off and we left that prize behind. It wasn't really trophy mounting quality, because the points were seven on one side and five on the other, but he hated to give up those antlers. I was glad to be rid of those large, dead eyes staring at me accusingly.

Al checked his watch. It was six-o-clock at night, turning dark and colder. We still had two tough miles to go to reach the car. We each dragged an eighty-pound section of venison meat. Much of the time we couldn't drag it through the closely rooted sagebrush, but had to muscle it up and over the top of the spidery growth, leaving flattened brush behind us. We stopped frequently to rest, both of us gasping for air and lungs aching.

"How are you doing, Mickey?" Al asked.

"Holy, Jesus. I'm tired. I'm hungry."

"Me too," he sighed.

I was so hungry I looked at the raw liver as a possibility for immediate nourishment.

"What a buck he was," I said.

"Yes he was. He's the best I ever shot." He paused. He wandered off in his memory. He came back to the moment and added, "I hope we're moving in a correct line to reach the road close to where the car is parked."

"I'll pray we are," I said.

"Do pray, Mickey."

With such a clear sky, I was sure God would hear me. The rough-surfaced rope was cutting my skinny hips. I reached down under my coat and shirt and felt blood. I reduced the pressure by using more hand strength and shifting the position of the rope frequently.

I reminded myself, "This burden I'm struggling with is more than a heavy chunk of deer meat to fill out a menu. I must hold my head up and meet this challenge. I must ignore the physical pain. There is much more to me than the world sees."

It turned colder. Millions of brilliant, pulsing stars filled the black sky. Thankfully, a half-moon provided enough light for us to see our way over the treacherous, rocky ground and tangle of sagebrush-roots.

I sweated from my effort and my sweat turned cold and clammy. Every part of me ached. I stumbled many times. The weight and bulk of the burden I was roped to helped me stay erect long enough to rebalance, and stay on my feet.

We reached the road four hours later. The car was only a hundred feet from the spot where we finally paused. Exhilarated, I caught my breath. I was exhausted, starved, and raw from rope burns.

I stood straight and stepped free of my cruel rope harness. I watched Al as he walked along the gravel roadway. Stiffly, he got in the car. Gratefully, the car started. He backed up to where I waited. With the last of our strength, we lifted each half of what remained of the deer in the trunk. He tied the trunk lid down. We climbed in the warming vehicle and headed home.

It was eleven o'clock when we arrived at the house. Virginia greeted us with relief, and irritation.

"I wanted to call the police, but I didn't have any idea where you'd be."

The hard truth was Al never wanted to be committed to a certain area for hunting. The conditions were always changing and the location of the deer changed with them. Which remote area we might hike to, always remained uncertain.

She cooked the fresh liver in a skillet, fried canned white potatoes in bacon grease, and heated canned peas. I was totally famished. No food ever tasted so good. When I finally crawled in my hallway cot and burrowed under the covers, my body continued to vibrate from stubborn cold and muscle fatigue. I now knew what the expression "cold to the bone" meant.

Peggy didn't wake up and rush out of her bedroom to greet us. She missed my triumphant return from a heroic exploit. I achieved a great victory and she wouldn't ever know about the courage I displayed.

Early the next morning, Al and I took the deer carcass to the local freezer rental facility where they butchered, packaged, and labeled one-hundred and thirty-five-pounds of venison. A winter's supply of roasts, steaks, chops and ground deer meat were safely stored in a rented freezer locker.

CHAPTER TWENTY-SEVEN

I worked as a helper on the Salvation Army truck picking up donations to sell at the thrift store. Some of the donated articles were usable. Some were trash people just wanted to get rid of. We took it all. Carrying items down steep, narrow stairways of buildings and up the ramp to the truck was hard work. We took out-dated appliances, stained mattresses, sagging couches, and scratch-marred dressers. I carried boxes and paper bags full of unidentified objects from people's houses and loaded them in the truck. We accepted anything and everything left at the curb for us. No dead bodies, please.

A recovering alcoholic driver and scrawny me struggled down a dim, creaking stairway with a heavy, ancient icebox. The pay for this job barely covered the cost of a hamburger, soda, and candy bar. I did have fun riding around in the truck with the sliding passenger door latch in the open position. As we searched for addresses, I stood on the bottom of the three steps, hung onto the door handle, and saw myself as a daring outrider on a speeding stagecoach.

"There's where our next pickup is, Bill."

When sober, the down and outers who found work at the Salvation Army store were usually okay people. As long as they treated me decently, I didn't worry about what sins brought them to their lowly, difficult condition in life.

My immersion in the Salvation Army way of life was deep. My stepsister Peggy and I traveled with Captain and Mrs. Owens to attend the graduation ceremonies of the year's new officers at the Salvation Army Training Center in San Francisco, California. It was a long six-hundred-fifty-mile drive in each direction.

We left Ogden in the Owens dark-blue, 1954 Ford station wagon. The official vehicle of the Ogden Center, it bore the Salvation Army logo on both front doors. The car sagged with six occupants inside, and a heavily loaded luggage rack on top. The Owens sat up front, Peggy and Jamie Lopez shared the middle seat, and I sat in the smaller back seat next to a girl named Ruby.

There was the thought Peggy, Jamie, or I might one day qualify as potential candidates to be officers in the Salvation Army. Supposedly, we were the only young people from the Ogden branch who possessed the required academic and character qualifications. The next big question would be how strong our devotion to the cause of saving wretched souls from the ruination of skid row was, and aiding unfortunate families living in poverty.

Ruby showed no desire or ability for a career so demanding and glorious. The trip was a mission of charity for her, a temporary escape from her wretched home life. She was from the poorest section of Ogden. She lived with her family in a dilapidated house in the white ghetto, the hellhole where the most impoverished of the city's Caucasians resided.

Ruby wore a well-worn, faded-pink dress she obtained at

the thrift store. Her grooming was haphazard, she tended towards plumpness, and her pale skin showed many freckles. I saw her as pretty in a girlish way. I overheard some cruel people whisper she was the lowest sort of white trash. They said she came from the most backwards of the backwoods. Even though I experienced constant approaches from sexual predators, and heard lots of gross conversations among boys my age, there were whispers about sexual abuse in her family I couldn't visualize.

Captain and Mrs. Owens planned to share the driving, and we started out at sunrise with high spirits. We traveled south, gaining a view of the shimmering Great Salt Lake on our right. We traversed Salt Lake City's wide and precisely laid out streets and passed the familiar, but always imposing Mormon Temple. This massive granite structure with six gleaming spires reached up toward the heavens and God. Despite its majesty, to me it was a monument to religious intolerance, and the wretched symbol of the people who ostracized me.

Westward on Route 40, we came closer to the shore of the Great Salt Lake and its once palatial resorts. The lake, through drought and evaporation, dramatically shrank in size. The now abandoned and dilapidated buildings became too distant from the salt-laden waters to have any usefulness as a tourist destination.

"I swam in the lake."

"You mean you floated in the lake."

"You don't want to swallow any of that saltwater."

"I didn't think I'd ever be able to rinse the salt from my swimming suit."

Directly ahead of us, the intimidating Great Salt Lake Desert awaited.

. . .

Through the reflection of sunlight, the desert we crossed became a land of lakes; beautiful blue, sparkling pools of water disappearing as you neared them. Further on the horizon, shimmering new lakes took their place. Those torturous visions of life-saving water couldn't ever be reached. Our history books in school claimed the mirages drove lost and thirsty pioneers and prospectors to madness.

The last of the barren, brownish-sand desert blended with and was replaced by the total whiteness of salt flats stretching to the horizon. On the salt flats the mirages were more frequent and the waters they projected were bluer and more tempting. I repeatedly found it difficult to believe the bodies of water just a few miles distant weren't real reservoirs filled with cool, refreshing water, and wonderful places to enjoy a cooling swim.

As we drove on, the salt flats disappeared behind us. Pale-gray, scrub-brush dotted desert and low, rolling hills filled the landscape.

Jackrabbits, with their ridiculously long ears, stood in sentinel poses near the roadway as we passed. Some bounded away to the safety of the desert scrub. Some were so confused, they jumped directly in the path of speeding vehicles and lay dead on and next to the roadway. I always hated the sight of roadkill. There was an endless stream of traffic barreling along in a hurry leaving many dead critters along this two-lane highway.

While sharing the cramped back seat of the station wagon, I became careless. Ruby placed her hand on mine and somehow, we were holding hands. The vehicle was already too warm inside for comfort and both our hands sweated. As we rolled across the boring desert, I wondered what the hell I was doing. I really wanted my hand free, but didn't know how to go about freeing it.

Much to my relief, we stopped in Wendover, just across the border in Nevada, for lunch at a small roadside cafe. She released my hand.

We all ate hamburgers and potato chips, and drank sodas. After I wolfed down my food, I looked out over the desert surrounding us. I marveled at the remoteness of the place. I also marveled that the state of Nevada was free of Mormon Church rule, and felt a wonderful sense of relief.

The Owens paid for everyone's lunch, but when it came time to purchase gum or mints, we were on our own. It turned out Ruby didn't have a single penny of pocket money with her. I handed her a dime so she could buy some sweets.

Before we got back in the car after lunch, Peggy and I were momentarily alone. "I noticed you gave Ruby a dime," she said. "Usually, Ruby would do anything for a dime. I mean anything, Mickey!"

Oh, God. Peggy noticed and criticized my actions. She questioned my judgment. I was horrified by my indiscretion. But she solved my dilemma.

I didn't hold hands with Ruby anymore. I maintained coolness towards her. I didn't talk to her. I did wonder a lot about the "anything" she'd do for a dime.

I snuck looks at Ruby. She was deeply hurt and it was my fault. I was still embarrassed by my mistake of treating Ruby like she could be my girlfriend. I made that terrible misjudgment in front of my stepsister Peggy, my truest, secret love. Still, I was surprised by the harshness of Peggy's judgment against Ruby. And, how much did Peggy know about the "anything" Ruby would do for a dime? I hated that I was so naïve. I hated that I was so ignorant about the "anything" Ruby would do.

At our next stop Ruby insisted on changing seats. Jamie

and I sat crowded in the back seat. Peggy and Ruby shared the middle seat. Both girls kept the largest possible distance between each other, and jealously guarded their tiny private spaces.

CHAPTER TWENTY-EIGHT

"Watch out!" Mrs. Owens shouted.

I startled awake from a fitful nap. The station wagon swerved. Everyone swayed with the sudden back and forth movement.

Darting out of a gully, a pack of four dogs crossed the road directly in front of us. It was too late to stop. There was a dull thud and a muted yelp. I looked back through the car's rear window and saw the dog we hit. It was desperately dragging its badly injured back half. The other three canines swarmed around it. At first, I thought they were concerned for their injured friend. Then I realized they were attacking their injured pack mate. All four dogs were skeletal thin. The injured member of the pack became food for the three survivors.

"There isn't anything we can do to help," Captain Owens said. "I'm really sorry. I couldn't avoid hitting it."

"That poor animal," Mrs. Owens lamented.

There were no signs of human habitation anywhere around

us. There were no hints the dogs were someone's beloved pets. All of us expressed sorrow and regret.

"I hate to see things like that," Peggy said.

Ruby wiped away tears.

"It happens sometimes," stoic Jamie said.

It took a while for the harsh reality of death to leave the vehicle. Slowly, nerves settled down.

I struggled to erase the sight of the pack attacking its fallen comrade and the wide, frightened eyes of the desperate, doomed victim. I focused on the reality of me, myself. I hadn't been hit by a car. I was safe. I remembered words I heard voiced many times by fellow Christians. There, but for the grace of God, go I.

The sight of Reno, Nevada, with the towering Sierra Nevada Mountains as a backdrop, was a welcome relief from the unending, monotonous scrubland we drove across.

We pulled in a busy and noisy truck-stop and slowly navigated past dozens of smoke-belching semis to the passenger-car area to gas up. Everyone exited the vehicle and gratefully stretched their legs. Despite the smells of gasoline, diesel fuel, and oil, the outside air was still a welcome change from the stuffy interior of the car.

Back on the road and experiencing a bumper to bumper passage through downtown Reno, we were entertained by a flood of bright, flashing casino lights. Festive gamblers crowded the wide sidewalks. There wouldn't be any gambling for us. We were dedicated Christians. We were also penny poor.

It'd been a hard-driving, 430-mile day. Everyone was exhausted beyond mere fatigue. On the western outskirts of Reno, we stopped at a cheap café for hamburgers. The Owens rented a room at a nearby, so-called economy motel. They shared the small room with Peggy and Ruby. Jamie and I slept in the station wagon.

After a miserable night in the cramped vehicle, I faced a mad scramble sharing the single bathroom in the seedy motel room with five other impatient people. Breakfast was coffee and pancakes at the same greasy-spoon café where we'd eaten our dinner of hamburgers.

Quickly, we were back on the road. Peggy was in a foul mood. She didn't like sharing the tiny, moldy bathroom. The ever-optimistic Owens still believed in our mission in San Francisco.

In an effort to restore our sagging spirits, Mrs. Owens led us in singing.

"Onward Christian soldier,

marching as to war."

We began the long climb up and over the Sierra Mountains.

"Go! Go!" We yelled encouragement as Captain Owens anxiously watched the temperature gauge of our overloaded vehicle.

The station wagon labored valiantly up the steep, curving highway as we approached Donner Pass.

This was my first visit to this famous part of the country. The immensity and beauty of the Sierra Mountains held me in awe. The variations in the colors and forms of the wind and water sculptured mountains was another American West wonder. Evergreen trees sprouted from a million crevices. It was my first experience of having my ears pop from elevation change. Damn. I hoped the damage wasn't permanent.

We made it to the top. We were over seven-thousand-feet above sea level.

On the descent, everyone worried about the capability of the braking system of our heavily-loaded station wagon. We passed slow moving semi-trucks whose brakes screamed in agony and left behind trails of smoke and the rotten smell of burning asbestos. Turnouts for runaway vehicles and remains of a couple of wrecked trucks showed the danger to be a harsh reality.

We made it to the bottom. Everyone sighed with relief. We didn't careen wildly out of control, catapult over a steep cliff, and fall screaming hundreds of feet to our bloody deaths. The Owens said God brought us over safely. God kept quite busy on this mountain passage, and he failed a few truckers and some old-time pioneers. But, we Christian soldiers, with God's selective help, conquered the mighty Sierra Mountains.

The earth leveled out ahead of us. We cruised confidently across the Central Valley of California. Only the capital city of Sacramento interrupted the miles of boring, flat farmland stretching to the horizon.

"San Francisco!"

It was a sparkling clear day. We drove across the Bay Bridge toward the magical city on seven hills. Ships and sailboats of every size plied the blue waters at the famous city's feet. A couple of large passenger liners decorated with colorful pennants were docked at the city's waterfront. I especially admired the big cargo ships, many with intriguing Oriental names, plowing across the bay. I imagined being a sailor who traveled to exotic ports throughout the world. The waterfront, with its many piers jutting out in the bay, would be where my sailor adventures of the future would launch from.

"Hey, there's Alcatraz! Al Capone was imprisoned there"

"Look! There's the Golden Gate Bridge!"

"A US Navy ship is passing under the bridge."

When the sunlight touched it, the Golden Gate Bridge did appear to be made of solid gold. In contrast to the deep blue background of the open ocean, every inch of the towering, suspension structure glowed with a rich, yellowish-red color.

The sun sparkled off the clean, white buildings climbing and descending the hills of San Francisco. What a great city to live in.

We took a sharply curving exit ramp from the bridge. We drove busy city streets, many with cable car tracks down the middle. Finally, we found our way to The Salvation Army Training College on Geary Avenue.

We were all car-weary travelers and happy to stretch out. We were directed to the nearby YMCA, where it was two people to a room, and nothing was fancy. It was much better than sleeping in a cramped car. Our goal here in San Francisco was to attend various sessions at the training college.

I found the speakers, and the subjects we listened to at the Training College painfully boring. I worried we wouldn't be allowed any time at all to be tourists in the colorful city of San Francisco. But, finally, we were released.

We tried to fit in as much sightseeing as our limited time, and even more limited budget, allowed.

We rode noisy, crowded, bell-clanging cable cars. We visited Chinatown where the plucked carcasses of ducks and chickens hung everywhere, and the language of the local Chinese was indecipherable. Produce of kinds I never imagined overflowed from sidewalk stalls. Elaborate ivory carvings, some requiring an entire elephant tusk, filled storefront windows.

We visited Fisherman's Wharf, where dead fish layered on ice stared at me accusingly. We couldn't afford to buy the shrimp cocktails to go. Tempting loaves of French bread were offered for sale. I really liked the fishing boats. I imagined being an expert crew member, with my boat surging fearlessly over choppy seas, headed for port with a prize catch of fish.

We watched mountain-high waves of gray fog roll in to envelop the city. The thick blanket of fog compressed all sound and made the sky seem like it was a mere twenty-feet above my head. The temperature plunged rapidly, and all of us shivered.

Alas, the time for tourism was brief. Back in the dining room of the College, we shared meals and conversation with the new Salvation Army Officers.

"It was really tough to make the commitment to be an officer," Ann said.

She was young and pretty and I fell in love with her. I had trouble seeing Ann spending her life singing hymns, shouting out sermons, and shaking a tambourine on some filthy, skid row street.

"You not only have the challenge of maintaining your faith, and your commitment," she continued. "You have to find a life partner who'll share the mission with you. You have to sustain that life partnership."

She sighed. The weight of the challenge made her shoulders sag. A fleeting moment of doubt clouded her face.

I wondered if I'd find a Salvation Army lassie like her to marry. It didn't seem likely.

"It's really difficult," she said. Her smile returned. "It'll take lots of prayer, but I know I can be successful."

I realized it wasn't going to be easy to be a servant of the Lord. Being a Salvation Army officer certainly wouldn't compare to the thrilling adventure of being a sailor aboard a mighty ship sailing the high seas. I loved the salty smell of the ocean and bustling harbors. I was attacked by feelings of doubt over whether I really had the calling and resolve to serve the Lord for the rest of my life.

On the long drive back home, the Sierras were still overwhelmingly majestic, and sometimes frightening. The Nevada desert was still desperately barren and boring. The mirages of shimmering blue lakes kept sprouting in the waste-land and tricking me into believing their lie. Fortunately, there were no more stray dogs to hit and kill. We did collide with and kill one jackrabbit. We smashed thousands of bugs to their deaths. The demise of the rabbit brought forth expressions of grief from Mrs. Owens, Peggy and Ruby.

The dust devils entranced me. Small ones formed and dissi-pated rapidly. Others were born and grew to thousand-foot heights, with funnels fifty-feet across. Those whirlwinds rotated closer and closer to the car as we sped down the two-lane road. The mini-cyclones threatened to grab and lift us up in the sky, and then let us go crashing back to earth. They did bring a bit of excitement to interrupt my growing apprehension over my return to dreaded Ogden, Utah.

San Francisco was exhilarating, colorful, and empty of threats. I imagined myself as an officer in the Salvation Army. I ministered for Jesus and saved wretched sinners. Preaching from the pulpit and hiding behind Jesus, I was safe from the bullies of the world.

To my mind, it'd become absolutely clear. For me, in Utah,

there was the Mormon world of oppression, and everywhere else, the non-Mormon world of freedom.

When we crossed the state line back to Utah, I saw myself in a striped prison uniform. I felt the heavy weight of iron shackles being locked onto my hands and feet. Religious intolerance was an evil force holding me in its unbreakable grip.

CHAPTER TWENTY-NINE

A knock at the front door interrupted a quiet evening. Always anticipating one of her wandering sons surprisingly appearing at her doorstep, Virginia rushed to answer it.

She opened the door. "Tommy," she exclaimed.

She pulled him inside and threw her arms around him. She hugged him like a long-lost son should be embraced. When she finally released him, she closed the door to the dark and cold outside world.

Bleary-eyed and unwashed, Tommy wore a colorful paratrooper uniform, which looked slept in. An apprehensive Al Davey shook his hand. My lovely stepsister, Peggy, embraced him with a warm, welcoming hug. Jesus Christ. She never showed any inclination to hug me at all. Goddamn her. Goddamn Tommy!

As the celebration quieted down, Tommy finally noticed me. He stared at me like he was trying to remember who the hell I was.

"Oh. It's Mickey, right?"

"Of course, it's Mickey," Virginia interjected. "Are you on leave from the Army, Tommy?" she asked hopefully.

"No. I quit."

"You quit?"

"Yeah, I quit."

"You can't just quit the Army."

"Well, I did."

"Are you AWOL?"

"I guess that's what they call it."

"You're in trouble, then?"

"I'm in trouble only if they find me."

"You're in trouble even if they don't find you, Tommy," Al reluctantly spoke up.

My oldest brother was AWOL from the 101st Airborne Division. I hadn't seen him for five years. After all the hard times we shared on the dangerous streets of Chicago, I hated how he treated me like I was nobody. I always knew he didn't like me, but it wasn't my fault I was so different from him.

Since he was a fugitive, Al Davey didn't want him staying at the house. He especially didn't want him around his beloved daughter, Peggy, who seemingly remained innocent.

"Please go talk to the police," Virginia pleaded with him. She placed a plate of warmed-up leftovers on the table in front of him. "The Army will probably be easy on you because of your age. Don't make it worse. We aren't going to hide you. You can't stay here."

"Sure, Mom, I understand. I don't want you to start worrying about me." He wolfed down the food and occasionally flashed his nothing-scares-me grin. "This venison is good, Al," he said as he chewed a mouthful of roasted deer meat.

Damn! I helped stalk, kill, gut, and drag that deer to the car. Nobody gives me credit for anything.

"They shouldn't have let you enlist, Tommy. You were only seventeen. I didn't give my permission."

"Good thing you gave your permission for me to be put away in that reform school when I was twelve-years-old, Mom."

"It wasn't a reform school, Tommy. It was Boys Town."

"You know what it was like inside that place?"

"I didn't know what else to do, Tommy. The judge said it was the best thing for you."

"Sure, Mom. Whatever you say is right."

My oldest brother had no intention of showing our mother any mercy.

Tommy didn't have any resources or friends in Ogden. After Virginia and Al fed him, they let him sleep on the floor overnight.

The next morning, Al drove him to Ogden police headquarters. Tommy confessed his situation. The Ogden Police locked him up to wait for the arrival of military police from Georgia. Being in jail at least gave him shelter and food.

Several days later, Virginia and I visited Tommy on the train, just before it left to take him back to Fort Benning, Georgia. The two Military Police, who arrived in Ogden to take him in custody, were armed with heavy nightsticks, and forty-five-caliber pistols. They kept a close watch on him. Tommy wore handcuffs and leg irons, but didn't appear bothered by his situation. He grinned and joked with us. I felt nausea from seeing him as a shackled prisoner. Even though he was only seventeen-years-old, I worried they'd put him in a brutal, military prison for the rest of his life. They'd beat him to a bloody pulp, and he'd die alone behind bars.

"I'm really worried about you," Virginia said. Her eyes misted over.

"Don't worry about me, Mom," smiling Tommy said. "I always take care of myself."

"I always worry about you."

"Yeah, you do, Mom. Sure."

"I really do, Tommy."

He ignored her pleading. He looked down at his shackled feet.

"Can I give him a hug, Corporal?"

"Go ahead, Mrs. Davey."

After her big hug, he and I exchanged a limp handshake. No brotherly love was evident.

Virginia shed real mother's tears as we watched the train leave the station.

I was sick thinking about high-walled prisons, barbed wire, and guards with deadly rifles.

I didn't understand how Peggy Davey could stand to have Virginia's strange sons drifting in and out of her life. Maybe it broke the boredom. At least Tommy and Ben broke the boredom. I knew Peggy wasn't impressed in the least bit by my existence.

Soon after Tommy was taken to Georgia as a military prisoner, he returned to Ogden. Since he was underage, the Army knew they screwed up by letting him enlist twice. They couldn't throw him in the brig and beat him into submission. He received a discharge from the paratroopers. They were probably glad to be rid of him.

He found work in Ogden as an auto mechanic. At least he'd

picked up a skill he liked while he was in Boy's Town when he was twelve-years-old. He now lived in a shabby room in a skid row hotel reeking from alcohol, and mildew. Occasionally, he visited us. Sometimes, I saw him around town.

On one of those days, he and I walked side by side along a sidewalk. In many ways, though I was a couple of inches taller than him, I still looked up to Tommy. He was handsome and muscular. He carried himself with a swagger. His dark hair was slicked back except for a tuft that fell onto his forehead. He decorated his biceps with tattoos. Damn. I didn't have enough biceps to tattoo. He built and drove hot rods. He did all the things I didn't have the guts to do. Always ready to rumble, Tommy didn't back down from anyone. He didn't hide from the bullies of the world the way I did.

Suddenly, as we strolled along, like a bolt of lightning flashing down from a dark sky, he said, "You know, Mickey, I don't really like you. I don't hate you. I just don't like you much."

Jesus Christ. Tommy blindsided and sucker punched me. As he continued in a dispassionate tone, I struggled to maintain my balance; to comprehend the words I heard.

"You're not a real Shafer, Mickey. Maybe, you're half a Shafer, but that's all. You don't even act like a half. No one knows who your father was. You're the reason the family broke up. You're the reason Dad called Mom a whore."

He looked at me with his missing-front-tooth grin. I didn't see hatred or anger. He simply told me his truth. He let me know those brotherly bonds I valued so highly, didn't exist for him.

"You weren't much of a fighter in Chicago, Mickey. You were mostly scared of being punched and hurt."

"No, I wasn't," I protested weakly. I knew I was afraid during the worst of our street fights and when we committed crimes. As we walked along, I tripped on the uneven sidewalk. I staggered, but quickly regained my balance.

"You are smart, though, Mickey. I'll give you credit there. Most of the time, I don't understand what the fuck you're talking about. But, you're too much of a goody-goody," he said with finality. He added, "You trip over your own feet too often."

I swallowed the bile rising up in my throat. I couldn't think of any words to reply. I really wanted my oldest brother to like, and respect me, but I didn't know how to convince him I was a worthwhile brother. I knew I wouldn't ever be as rebellious and tough as him.

We stopped at a corner grocery store so he could buy a package of Dentyne gum. He gave me one piece and stuffed the rest in his mouth. He acted as if the words he just threw in my face were of no importance. He was just clearing the air. I felt like I fell into the freezing abyss again. Cold ice blocked my intestines. I struggled to maintain my equilibrium. I didn't want to trip, and stumble again. Not while I walked next to my oldest brother.

"I chew a package of this gum once a week," he said. "It's great for your teeth, Mickey. It's faster, and cheaper than using a toothbrush. You should try it."

"I will," I choked on my words. "I've seen the commercial on television."

There was a benefit in his contempt for me. We never touched each other except for a couple of limp, insincere handshakes. He kept his hands off me, whereas he loved to wrestle to submission and punch our brother, Ben.

A week later, Tommy told me he needed my help. Hope surged through me. Maybe, my oldest brother didn't really mean what he said about not liking me. Maybe, he really considered me a bona-fide family member.

"I'll meet you in front of your house around ten tonight, Mickey. We'll need the little kid's wagon that used to be Peggy's."

It was a half-moon lit night when he pulled up to the front of the house in his rumbling hot-rod, Ford pickup truck.

"I'll park around the block, Mickey." My hopes always soared when he addressed me by my name. The noise of his truck's engine he rebuilt with his own hands almost drowned out his voice. "I'll meet you down at the corner."

I met him and we walked seven blocks to the garage where he worked. I pulled the little, red wagon behind us.

He unlocked the back door to the garage. He flipped on the overhead fluorescent lights. Stark-white brightness flooded the shop crowded with tools, auto parts, and autos being repaired or rebuilt. He positioned the garage jack under a low-riding hot rod decorated with flowing, multicolored flames painted along its sides.

"The owner sold me the transmission from this thing. I have to remove it outside of work hours." Lying face up on the creeper, he pushed himself under the car.

"Hand me the 9/16 socket, Mick."

Moving as efficiently as a surgeon's highly trained assistant, I handed him each tool he requested.

Tommy worked rapidly. After he lowered the transmission onto a couple of thick shop-rags placed on the concrete floor, we carefully pulled it out from underneath the hot rod. We lifted it up in the child's wagon. The weight of the transmission strained the limits of the little wagon and my underdeveloped muscles. Tommy grinned triumphantly as he turned off the lights, and we squeezed out the door.

It took both our strengths to push and pull the wagon and its cargo along the uneven sidewalk. We maneuvered the wagon down over curbs, and up over curbs. To lift the transmission up and in the back of his pickup truck seemed an impossible task. Thankfully, Tommy was incredibly strong. I stayed with the effort, and sensed his approval.

"Thanks a lot, Mick."

"Anytime you need me, Tommy. I'm always glad to help you."

"Hey, Mick. I'd like you to go to work with me in the morning. I'll pick you up at seven."

"Okay, Tommy. I'll see you then." I was feeling really good about our brotherhood. It took a lot of scrubbing to get the grease off my hands, and my back was sore from lifting the heavy transmission, but it was a small price to pay for my oldest brother's positive recognition.

We met as planned in the morning. When we walked in the garage shortly afterwards, there was an agitated conversation in progress.

"Some son-of-a-bitch stole the transmission out of Bill's car," Tommy's boss said angrily as he turned to look at us. "And there's no sign of a break-in."

"Man, that's fucked up," Tommy declared with great sincerity.

The boss-eyed Tommy suspiciously. So did Bill, and the other mechanic who worked at the garage.

"Man, I tell you, that's a really fucked-up situation," Tommy emphasized. As the heated discussion continued, Tommy flashed me a knowing look.

"Well, I think I'll go, Tommy." I was extremely uncomfortable. I hated standing next to my oldest brother and being a suspected burglar. I was his accomplice. Just like him, I was a hardcore thief. I feared being found out and going to jail.

"Sure," Tommy nodded at me. "I'll see you later, Mickey."

I wanted to believe otherwise, but I began to understand Tommy was a master of "Midnight Auto Parts." Stupid me! He only wanted my presence at the garage that morning to distract attention from himself.

As I thought about my oldest brother, I told myself we were at least half-brothers. We shared the same mother. But, the way people joked about mixed up babies at the hospital, I couldn't be absolutely sure about any of my parentage. Maybe the hospital switched me with some rich people's kid. I might really be a high-class kid who was cast out of his rightful place in a mansion. I was supposed to inherit a rich and powerful corporation. Instead, I was a penniless outcast wandering aimlessly through a merciless wilderness. Why the hell didn't God prevent such an awful thing from happening to me?

CHAPTER THIRTY

Much to my surprise, Tommy came to church services at the Salvation Army. Then, I saw him checking out the young females in attendance. He was hunting.

He focused on Diana, a full-fleshed, busty, and ripe sixteen-year-old. I saw her as fat, but since she was young, I guess Tommy must have seen her as all lusty flesh. Shy and uneducated, she had a squarish face, with large brown eyes, and full lips. She was dirt poor, and vulnerable. My oldest brother zeroed in on her instinctively. He was the hungry wolf in pursuit of the naïve, stray lamb.

Tommy made his move on her. He impregnated her. A shotgun wedding rapidly followed.

He moved to Ogden's poor-white-trash slums to live with her in her mother's crowded, ramshackle house. In that ignored section of Ogden, the streets weren't paved, and city services were non-existent. The houses were patched together with whatever cheap or throwaway materials were available. It was an unorganized mixture of small weathered frame houses, tin-roofed unpainted shacks, and decaying house trailers. The potholed, dirt streets swarmed with ragged, dirty-faced kids. As soon as they could crawl, children were turned out to their playground of junked cars, broken appliances, and piles of trash.

Diana shunned the outside world. She stayed inside her mother's dimly-lit house, watched her small black and white television, and consumed boxes of the cheapest brand of chocolate-covered cherries.

One day, when I stopped by the house looking for Tommy, she'd just finished nursing her baby. She was buttoning the top of her dress when she came to the front door. I saw ten greasy fingerprint smudges on her bulging breasts. I guess it was the mark of being married to an automobile mechanic. Tommy came home for what he called a "nooner."

"Tommy's at the garage, Mickey," she said. "You just missed him."

"Thanks, Diana."

She held her two-month-old baby close to her generous body. Through the sagging, raggedy screen door, I smelled the stench of baby shit and urine.

"Would you like to come in, Mickey?"

"No thanks, Diana. I need to get to the garage to see Tommy." Dirty little neighborhood kids swarmed around me, and one of them grabbed my hand. I wanted to escape this hellhole as fast as possible. Damn. I wasn't being much of a warm-hearted Christian.

My almost girlfriend, Ruby, lived in this wretched place. She got pregnant, quit school, and stopped coming to the Salvation Army church services. I was beginning to understand a terrible truth. If I wasn't careful, I could end up in a similar, hopeless pit myself.

When I saw Tommy at the garage, he made a joke about being squirted in the face with mother's milk and he didn't like the taste of it. I wanted to erase everything about my oldest brother and his way of living from my mind, but I couldn't. We both came from the same wretched beginning in the slums of Chicago. At the very least, we were born from the same woman.

While I was at the Salvation Army Chapel helping to prepare for evening service, Mrs. Owens asked me to deliver a message to Captain Owens. I started up the stairway to the second floor living quarters. Halfway up, I saw him through a partially open door. I heard his preacher's voice thunder angrily. I saw him pull his belt out of his trouser loops.

"How many times have I warned you, Carol?"

I backed up a step. I didn't want to see anything I wasn't supposed to see. Whenever I heard adult anger directed at children, a surge of horror and revulsion always swept over me. My guts twisted into a painful knot, and I wanted to flee for safety.

"No, Daddy, don't!" Carol cried out. "Please, Daddy. I didn't do anything wrong."

I couldn't avert my eyes. I saw in a flash the overhead swing of the wide belt. I heard the sound of the thick, leather strap hitting Carol's thin legs. I stood frozen in place. I wanted to turn away, and run from this terrible scene, but I couldn't move. My body quit obeying me. I couldn't make myself retreat. I was forced to listen to the terrifying beating.

"I'm sorry, Daddy," Carol cried out in her frightened, childish voice, as she pleaded for mercy.

The impact of the belt upon her shaking body continued. Each lash produced a tearful cry of agony.

I watched his arm rise into the air again. I watched his belt swing in its vicious arc, to flay the skin of his fragile female child.

"Please stop, Daddy," her wretched voice pleaded.

I heard the belt's impact on her thin arms. I heard her childish cry of pain.

Filled with revulsion, dismay, and feeling terribly sick, I finally found the strength to turn away. I stumbled down the stairway. I was in shock. I wished I had my rifle and could kill the bastard.

That evening's sermon was one of the Captains most fervent. His voice resonated with great power, and unwavering conviction. Carol sat near and below his pulpit in a chair facing the congregation. She wore a blue frock with short puffed sleeves, and a short skirt over a white petticoat. I saw welts on her arms and legs. She was red eyed, withdrawn. The emptiness in her eyes was truly frightening.

She was so pretty, so slight, so delicate. I wondered what terrible sin she'd committed, to earn such a brutal whipping.

Slowly, I sensed the real truth. It wasn't about sin or wrongdoing. I witnessed hateful, cruel, perverted, child abuse. Her father was a disciple of the Devil. He was evil hiding behind the name of Jesus Christ. His female child was the stand-in for his unfaithful wife. He enjoyed his child's helplessness. He enjoyed his child's pain.

"Don't, don't, don't ever trust anyone," reverberated through my mind.

Frictions developed. Friendships fractured. Faith faltered among the congregation. Gossip swirled. Tales of marital cheating, casual sex and sexual harassment were loudly whispered about.

Virginia disclosed there was a proposal of wife swapping. She demanded we quit the Salvation Army. Al and Peggy didn't offer resistance.

I witnessed God's messenger brutally beating his frail daughter. What I saw was more than enough for me to fear and abhor both God, and all his messengers. I never wanted to walk into a chapel, or hear a preacher's voice again. Poor Carol didn't have any choice.

I always harbored doubts about those shouting out, and sermonizing for compassion and mercy. I saw too many of those preaching kindness and gentleness failing to live up to those ideals in their daily life. Many times, they were the most brutal of humans.

People overflowing with religious conviction liked to quote, "Spare the rod and spoil the child."

I personally lived with more than enough of the cruelty espoused in the Holy Bible. Naomi read her bible before and after she beat me. Humans looked for any excuse to brutalize, and dominate children, and any other helpless victims.

This ended my latest adventure with organized religion. I didn't feel any desire to travel that twisted path again. I wasn't sure if I ever would. My trust in all religion was seriously diminished. I now doubted there was any purpose in praying to Jesus or God for help against the world's hate and abuse. I now doubted Jesus or God even existed. Too much evil prospered and hid behind their names.

With the Salvation Army out of her life, Virginia found a new mission. She took in her care, a two-year-old, American Indian girl. The poor creature's brain was severely scrambled by her Ute mother's heavy drug use during pregnancy.

"We don't hold much hope for her future," the social services lady said. "But, any time in a real home, is so much better than institutionalization."

Virginia brought the hopeless child into the family on a full-time basis. We all dealt with the disruption in our own way.

I spent most of my time away from the house either working or searching for work, so I easily avoided the shit smells and the screaming fits. The most unsettling experience was seeing the little girl bang her head against the walls and floor.

Peggy wasn't happy about this new addition to the family, but didn't complain.

Al Davey went along with anything that appeared to make Virginia happy.

My mother stayed unfazed by the never-ending difficulties of caring for this terribly abused toddler. She lavished her time, and her love on the crippled product of human ignorance. Nobody knew for sure, the total sum of the horrors unloved Penny had already endured from her drug-addicted mother.

CHAPTER THIRTY-ONE

I was fifteen-years-old and needed serious work and money. Most of the best jobs in Ogden, Utah weren't available to non-Mormons, but I heard pinsetters were in demand at the local bowling alley. I walked to the Ben Lomond Lanes on Washington Boulevard and approached Dennis, the man in charge of hiring setters.

"I'd like to learn to be a pinsetter, sir."

"It's a tough job." Dennis looked at me skeptically. I didn't blink or waver. "You're pretty skinny, kid."

"I've done lots of tough work, sir. I'd really like to try."

"Well, go on back and watch the pinsetters at work. Then we'll talk."

I entered the noisy and poorly lit machinery area of the bowling emporium. I saw pin boys pop up and down like targets in a shooting gallery. I watched them bend over to pick up sixteen-pound bowling balls, lift the black spheres up onto the return chute, and apply a good shove so the balls rolled all the way back to the bowlers. The constantly moving setters picked up two to three pins with each hand, and noisily slammed them in their proper place in the pin rack. They pulled the cord to lower the rack. They moved quickly to repeat each motion in the second alley they were responsible for. I received a couple of curious looks, but mostly, I was ignored. They looked like a tough bunch. I looked at my hands. My hands weren't big and were soft. I walked back up front to talk to Dennis.

"I'd really like to try, sir."

"Okay," he said impatiently, "I'll put your name on the bottom of my list. If I get a couple of kid bowlers, I'll give you a chance. What's your name?"

"Mickey."

I watched to make sure he wrote my name down.

"Okay," he said. "See. There." He pointed at and tapped the list with his finger "Your name is written right there. Mickey is at the very bottom."

"Thank you, sir."

I waited. Soon he called my name. I got small jobs setting pins for kid bowlers. I learned quickly. I got jobs setting pins for awkward, adult bowlers. I learned to be more efficient. I worked faster. I got jobs setting for the better adult bowlers. Mostly males, they had no patience with slow or incompetent pinsetters. Dennis was impressed. The wage for setting pins was ten cents a game. One penny for each frame. I hoped nobody needed the third ball in their tenth frame.

I lifted the sixteen-pound ball chin high to get it up onto the return chute. I shoved it with all my strength. I spread my fingers as wide as possible to pick up two and sometimes three pins with each hand. I lifted the pins and slammed them in their proper place in the pin rack. I lowered the rack.

I was good at setting pins. I rapidly progressed up the list. I graduated to setting leagues, the big money. A league consisted of two teams of five bowlers, with three games for each competitor, a total of thirty games played at high speed. I earned a whole three dollars for a few hours work. And usually, I got tips.

On Saturdays, the leagues ran from ten-am until twelve-thirty and from one until three-thirty in the afternoon.

In a dramatic start to each league, the first competitors lined up and took their bowlers stance. They maintained the pose like a row of ancient Greek archers. Except for an occasional cough, or throat clearing, total silence enveloped the lanes.

"Bowlers, start your games," a voice boomed over the loud-speaker system.

Carefully measured footsteps pattered. Bowler's bodies bent at the waist. Arms swung in exaggerated arcs. Bowling balls were released and landed with a whisper on the polished wood lanes. Thump, thump, thump. The sixteen-pound spheres sounded like a low rumble of approaching thunder. The heavy plastic balls crashed into the patiently waiting red and white wooden statues. The merciless balls sent shocked tenpins flying in every direction.

With little kid or incompetent adult bowlers, the aimless ball often fell in the gutter, landing with a dull thud in the padded pit. Unskilled bowlers made my job easy.

From age fourteen to sixty, local boys and older men worked the pits. It was highly unlikely any of the setters were Mormon. The Mormon boys were hired in the best jobs in town. Believers in Joseph Smith, and Brigham Young, existed at a much higher level of regard in Utah than non-believers. Pinsetters were mostly poor white trash, and I suspected in some people's eyes, I was poor white trash.

Many of the older-men who worked the lanes were hobo types traveling the country from bowling alley to bowling alley. Most carried pint bottles of whiskey, pouches of tobacco, and packets of rolling papers in their pockets. The whiskey was perfect medicine for the aches and pains suffered from bending and lifting bowling balls, and being hit by flying tenpins. Usually, each pin boy set two alleys, and the space to stand between the alleys was narrow. Fat people didn't work back there. Softies didn't last long.

I gained speed and durability. Soon, I always worked both leagues, which was a grand total of sixty games. For my effort, I earned six dollars plus usually a twenty-five-cent or half-dollar tip from each team, as happy bowlers rolled quarters down the alley. Sometimes, I needed to crawl past the pins and out onto the alley to retrieve the quarters. I often got a standing ovation. I took a big bow, and my act sometimes brought another quarter or two.

After leagues were finished on weekends, I worked regular bowling until midnight. I put in many long, fifteen-hour days on Saturdays, Sundays and holidays. On one busy Saturday, I made fifteen bucks, a fortune for skinny me.

No one was going to steal, or cheat me out of my hard-earned money. I lived in plenty of bad situations, so I stayed a step ahead of the bullies and thieves who worked in the bowling alley. I didn't trust anyone. I knew how to use the so-called, law-abiding people of the world, as a shield against the riff-raff.

A pudgy, mean-faced kid, about sixteen-years-old, decided to harass me. Whenever we were close, he bumped me.

"Watch where you're walking, Bones," he smirked.

I attempted to avoid him, but it wasn't easy to dodge creeps in the tight quarters of the bowling alley pits.

"The only reason you get so much work, Bones, is because you're an ass kisser."

I ducked around him.

"Go smooch it up with Dennis, Bones."

The Ben Lomond Lanes were real tight with the Ogden police. Out front in the customer area, the management didn't tolerate crap from anybody. I spent most of my waiting-for-assignment-time there. I stayed within sight of law-abiding people and avoided hanging out with bad people. My nemesis, Pudgy, was a lazy bastard, who hated hard work, and eventually quit. I knew there'd always be another bully.

My biggest challenge was walking home after late nights of setting pins. Even though I was used to traveling in the dark, dodging in and out of shadows, and outmaneuvering predators, I never turned a corner without being alert for danger.

Back in the pits it was bend and lift, again and again, time after time. Above all else, I didn't want to become careless and drop a sixteen-pound bowling-ball on my feet and break bones. Tenpins constantly bounced off my legs and I could easily endure that. I picked up two or three pins in each hand and slammed them in the metal rack without pinching my fingers. Hopefully, I placed them in the right slot, so I could lower the rack on the remaining, standing pins. Sometimes the rack jammed on a misaligned pin. I pulled the cord to raise it, bent and reached to place all the pins on their exact spot, and then pulled the cord again to lower the rack. They didn't make the cords out of smooth rope. My hands toughened up quickly. I held onto my great job.

. . .

The nighttime bowlers were often drinkers having more fun boozing than bowling. Bozos showed off for their buddies or girlfriends. Those idiots could be deadly dangerous. One night, I bent over to pick up pins. I felt air move as a sixteen-pound bowling ball passed within an inch of my skull. My scalp tingled. Jesus Christ. I came really close to being killed. Damn. My anger rose up in a volcanic eruption. The asshole bowler came close to crushing my skull. He nearly ended my life because of his carelessness. From my place in the pit, I threw the ball back up the center of the alley. The stupid bowlers yelped and knocked over beer cans as they dodged the black, sixteen-pound ball rattling around in their sitting area. I surprised the hell out of those fools.

"You fucking assholes!" I shouted up the alley.

"Jesus," the guilty, drunken bowler shouted back. "Sorry."

The moron didn't know how young and skinny I was. He didn't call my bluff personally. The word on the street was pin boys could be dangerous.

"Some of those pin-boys carry switchblade knives or handguns. They're a bunch of hardened criminals."

The almost-killer went up to the front counter to complain. The night counterperson probably told him he'd talk to the crazy pinsetter. He wouldn't though. Finding good pinsetters wasn't easy.

I ate at the bowling alley restaurant. They served delicious cheeseburgers with onions, tomato, lettuce, pickle, mayo, and ketchup. I always added a large order of French fries with lots of ketchup, and a large glass of Coca Cola over ice. I topped off my wonderful meal with a slice of apple, or cherry pie, a la mode.

With a full stomach, I sat back, and waited for my name to

be called. I didn't have to wait long. I was a star, a fast and nearly perfect pinsetter.

I loved the atmosphere of the bowling alley. I liked the bright lights, happy voices, and constant, noisy activity. Only white people were permitted to bowl. No Blacks, Mexicans, or Indians allowed. That didn't seem right. My mother's father, my own grandfather, was half-Cherokee. He was a kind man, and although we hadn't spent much time together, I liked him. There weren't many gentle people in the world, so he was a rarity. They wouldn't let him bowl here, and some people would call him a dirty, thieving redskin.

There wasn't much tobacco smoking seen from the customers because of the Mormon religion's rule against it. The pinsetters smoked in the alley behind the building, one place I stayed away from.

"Mickey," Dennis yelled. "Take alleys nine and ten."

"I've got them."

One Saturday, Dennis was short of setters for a men's league. I and another fast worker covered three lanes each. We climbed out of our own pit to set the extra lanes. Sharing a small pit with another setter was hard and dangerous, but we did it. I was elated and ate two cheeseburgers that evening. One of the old-timers from off the road sat at the table across from me, eating his cheeseburger.

"How you doing with the Mormons, kid?"

"Not too good."

"I was married to a Mormon lady, but I always stayed a Jack Mormon."

"What's a Jack Mormon?"

"That's a Mormon who doesn't obey any of the church's stupid fucking rules."

"You didn't believe---

"Joseph Smith was an illiterate, lying, treasure hunter. The Book of Mormon he wrote is the biggest pile of crap ever put down on paper. I don't believe the Bible either, but at least it contains some decent writing." After glancing around looking for possible informers, he downed a long swig from the pint of booze he pulled out of his pocket.

The bowling alley job was much better than when I went to the Ogden labor center to find work. I showed up at five-thirty in the morning, and waited in a crowd of poor whites and poor Mexicans, who didn't want to be close to each other. We were all competing for day jobs picking cherries or tomatoes. The growers arrived in their noisy, dust-covered vehicles, looked the hopefuls over carefully, and pointed a finger at their choices. The lucky ones separated themselves from the crowd, and climbed in a van jammed with too many people already. Ahead lay a miserable, bone-jarring ride over pot-holed, dusty dirt-roads, and fields, to distant jobsites. It was difficult to breathe through all of the potent body odors in the van, then, some crude, foul person would fart silently, and smirk as everybody tried to breathe past the nasty stink.

I was so glad to get out of the cramped, beat-up, old van.

Carrying a battered metal pail in one hand, I climbed a narrow, flimsy ladder that bent and wobbled dangerously from my weight.

"Pick all the cherries at the very end of the branches, kid!" the foreman yelled. "You can't move to another tree until this one is completely picked. Get every single cherry!"

I left the ladder behind as I climbed higher in the rough-barked tree. I climbed further out onto the too-thin for my weight branches. I reached as far as my arms would stretch.

The limbs bent, shook, and threatened to break. I was sure I'd fall thirty-feet to the ground, and break every bone in my skinny body.

Other days, I stooped low to the ground, as I bent at my waist to pick tomatoes in vast tomato fields. Laboring under the blazing hot sun, I crabbed along at my top speed. My arms and hands reached to pick tomatoes, as I avoided stepping on squashed, rotting fruit littering the rows. Mosquitoes, gnats, and a million other bugs swarmed over any exposed part of my body. When it was time to stand up, I didn't believe my back would ever straighten out.

I hated picking cherries and tomatoes. I hated field labor. No work would ever top my job at the bowling alley. I believed working on those lanes would give me a great career, and a good financial future.

I made my first ever visit to a dentist. It cost me three-dollars for a small filling, and five-dollars for a big filling. A health check by a school nurse scared me enough I was willing to spend my hard-earned money for dental care.

"If you don't fix your teeth, they'll rot away. You'll be toothless by the time you're thirty-years-old."

I took myself to the dentist's office, and climbed up in the dreaded chair, for painful shots and nerve-rattling drilling. The dentist delivered a gentle, but firm lecture about brushing and dental hygiene.

With my hard earned dollars, I bought a .308 caliber, Savage Model 99, lever-action rifle at the local gun shop. The beautiful weapon cost me one-hundred and five-dollars. I loved my shiny new gun. I could shoot with the best during deer hunting season.

. . .

Men carrying clipboards and scribbling madly showed up at Ben Lomand Lanes. They took measurements, conversed among themselves, and ignored us pinsetters as if we didn't exist.

"They're bringing those fucking machines in," one of the old, itinerant setters grumbled.

The bowling alley shut down. Signs hung on the exterior of the building bragged about remodeling, and the bright new future with automatic pinsetters.

My career as a pinsetter ended. I was terribly depressed. But I learned something about myself. I was a good worker. Knowing I was a good worker made me a different person. It gave me self-confidence. Most employers liked good workers. I had value. If I found an escape from Mormon religious intolerance and lived in a free society, there wasn't any limit to my future.

CHAPTER THIRTY-TWO

On a deer-hunting expedition, Al Davey and I ventured to a sheepherder's remote camp high in the Wasatch Mountains. We drove through unknown country and the dirt roads were snow-packed over a layer of thick ice. Our slow progress in his clumsy, old Pontiac was slippery and risky. In this rough wilderness, a person didn't want to slide in a ditch and get stuck without communication to the outside world. There weren't any phone booths nearby. A landmark to guide us on our route was a moss-covered boulder at one mileage point, and a downed tree was another signpost. Luckily, we reached the camp. It was set in a beautiful mountain meadow surrounded by snow-laden evergreen and aspen trees.

Dave, the sheepherder, lived in this primitive setting in a tent wagon. His only company consisted of two shaggy mountain-horses, four super-tough sheep dogs, and five-hundred head of sheep. A deep snowfall blanketed the higher mountains, and he was forced to move his camp and the sheep down from the highest pastures to this more accessible, lower location.

We shared lunch with Dave in his tent wagon. The three of us barely fit in his tiny, cramped home. He served elk steaks, fried canned potatoes, and canned peas. His compact wood stove cooked the food quickly, and the heat it threw off made me remove my winter coat immediately.

Around thirty-five-years old, Dave was a rugged, handsome, cowboy type with a friendly, open manner. In my eyes, he was a heroic westerner. Sheep herding was a difficult and lonely job. He welcomed our visit.

"There's great hunting country around here," he assured us.

"This is the best campsite meal I've ever eaten, Dave," Al said.

I added my praise.

Al brought along two fifths of bourbon as a gift. A grateful Dave opened a bottle as we ate. Al wasn't a serious drinker, but he joined Dave for a shot of potent whiskey.

Dave carried the opened bottle of booze in his coat pocket as we set out on our hunt. I proudly carried my new Savage .308 caliber, lever-action rifle.

"Nice rifle, Mickey," Dave said. "You'll be able to knock down a big buck with it."

"Thanks, Dave. I hope so."

The countryside glowed with a fresh layer of snow, and the branches of the evergreen, and aspen trees sagged under the weight. The cold air was crisp with freshness. All three of us exhaled clouds of mist as we labored through knee-high drifts. I imagined being five-thousand-years in the past, and we were the first humans to ever step foot onto this part of the earth.

Al and Dave continued sharing nips from the bottle of whiskey, and didn't seem totally focused on hunting.

"Talk about warming up the belly," Dave commented.

Despite the deep snow, I surged forward as quickly and quietly as possible. Soon, I couldn't see or hear Al and Dave. I was totally alone in a prehistoric world.

I saw four deer about one-hundred yards ahead of me. They were cautiously emerging from a large clump of aspen. I froze in my tracks.

I considered waiting for Al and Dave, but I raised my rifle. I tried to hold my .308 steady, and sight in on the handsome buck leading the group. My body vibrated. My gun wavered. I was sighted in when I pulled the trigger. The blast filled the silence. The recoil of my rifle threw me off balance. I quickly recovered and levered in another round. The deer bounded away through the deep snow. I fired a wild shot in their direction. They were quickly out of sight.

Al and Dave appeared over the hill behind me.

"Did you get one?" Dave yelled.

"I don't think so," I shouted back. "I think I missed."

"Maybe they were out of range," Al said sympathetically when they caught up to me.

"Probably," I replied with disappointment.

"Buck fever," Dave said to Al with a chuckle.

"Could've been," Al replied quietly with a grin.

"Let's go over and make sure none were wounded," Dave said.

Damn. If only I could've shot my rifle without shaking. I had to admit they might have been too far away for me to hit one. Maybe, I needed a scope. Maybe, I wasn't too great of a deer hunter.

When we reached the aspen, there weren't any signs of fresh blood, just tracks of the fleeing deer.

"There won't be any more deer through here today," Dave

said. "Let's head back to camp. I've already had a few too many nips of whiskey."

Neither Al nor Dave seemed especially disappointed. Maybe my episode of buck fever would be quickly forgotten.

Back at camp, I tried to entice the four sheep dogs to play. They sat patiently a few feet away, blinked their puzzled eyes, and kept close track of my silly contortions. They listened to my childish words with interest, but kept their distance. Playing games with humans, they didn't seem to understand. Working sheep, and obedience to the herder, was their only life.

On the drive back to civilization, I imagined living the life of a sheepherder. It was another possible future for me.

The experiment with the social-welfare ward, Penny, ended. She lived as a member of the family, everyone was kind to her, and we all tolerated the difficulties she presented. Virginia finally admitted exhaustion. No amount of love, no amount of patience, could change the downward course of this unfortunate human's life. Twenty-four-hour vigilance was becoming required to keep her from destroying herself. The head banging proved too devastating a nightmare to live with.

Penny was returned to her life of institutional care.

Virginia grieved over the loss of this mentally-crippled stray she made part of her life. She lavished all the love she could draw on to reach Penny, but it was proven hopeless. I didn't understand why she made the effort.

CHAPTER THIRTY-THREE

*I*n my nightmare, Satan grabbed my shoulder. He pulled me down in his blazing inferno of hell. Ragged, blistered sinners pushed Bibles in my face and screamed, "Non-believer! You will join us!"

"Mickey. Wake up, Mickey. It's Mom." Through my fog of sleep, I barely comprehended her whispered words.

I struggled to wakefulness. I saw her hovering above me in the semi-darkness.

"Mickey," she continued in a whisper. "Be real quiet. Get dressed. Pack all your clothes in your suitcase. You and I are leaving this place."

I sat up. I recognized Al's loud snoring coming from his and her bedroom. He always slept soundly, and there was little chance he'd hear what was happening. Then, I remembered Peggy in her room. She also was a sound sleeper.

"I'm awake," I muttered.

"Get your stuff together," she whispered with more urgency. "Be very quiet."

I didn't have my own dresser, so I always kept my clothes

and other possessions under my cot in my suitcase. I dressed and jammed what was left of my hard-earned pin-setting money in my jean pockets. I owned very little and realized I'd have to leave my deer rifle and bicycle behind. I really didn't want to go down this road again with my mother, but I didn't know how to object.

We crept down the stairs to the first floor and quietly snuck out the front door.

"I called a cab. It should be here soon," she whispered in a panicky voice.

It was cold and foggy and she noticeably shivered. Her hands trembled. Fear of being discovered, and stopped by Al, was pushing her to the brink of full scale panic. I didn't want to witness her having a nervous breakdown, so I tried to be a calming influence.

"Where're we going?" I quietly clapped my freezing-cold hands together.

"We're going to Saint Louis, Mickey. We're going to my mother's place."

She relaxed a bit in the cab to the Greyhound bus station. In the early morning darkness and dense fog, the sign on the depot glowed with an eerie, green pallor. Slushy snow on the ground immediately chilled my feet as we walked to the double-entry door. Our footsteps echoed loudly across the marble floor of the high-ceilinged interior. With shaky hands, she counted out money to buy two tickets from the slow moving, bleary-eyed ticket agent. We sat on a hard, high-backed bench seat to wait. She jumped at every sound of a car approaching and passing the station. It was a short, but nerve-wracking time inside the nearly empty terminal, before we boarded an eastbound bus.

There were only three other passengers, an old couple and what looked like a rancher.

"We're on our way." She sighed with relief as we settled in our seats. After what seemed like forever, the bus backed out. I had the window seat and acted as the trusty lookout. I didn't see any sign of pursuit.

The driver dimmed the interior lights. The bus groaned loudly through gear shifting as we picked up speed and merged onto the two-lane highway. A cloud of diesel fumes dissipated behind us. It now seemed possible we'd be successful in her flight from Al Davey. My mother was well practiced in this game. When I was a small child, she hitch-hiked hundreds of miles on open highways with me and my three brothers in tow. The child-hood excitement of flight and escape was wearing thin with me.

She leaned back in her seat, let out a big sigh, and closed her eyes. I looked out in the night. I watched the last lights of civilization flicker by and disappear behind us. Soon, darkness was in command. Glittering stars vibrated in the night sky. The light from a half-moon reflected off the thin layer of snow covering the desolate, sagebrush-dotted countryside.

She turned to me with a look of worry.

"I took a bunch of pills, Mickey. I was so afraid we wouldn't get away from him."

Oh, no, I thought to myself. "Are you going to die?"

"I don't know, Mickey. I don't think so."

Holy, Jesus. What if she died right here, aboard this bus, while she sat next to me?

"I'm going to the restroom," she mumbled.

She wobbled when she stood up. She unsteadily worked her way back to the rear of the bus. She stayed in the lavatory a long time. Finally, the door opened and she emerged. She navigated the aisle more steadily as she returned to her seat next to me. Even though she didn't smell of puke, I was sure she threw up plenty.

"I feel much better now." She touched my arm. I kept my reactive flinch buried inside of me. She settled in her seat.

I hoped she wouldn't die. How the hell would I deal with her corpse, and funeral? I enjoyed seeing the monster Naomi buried, but I didn't think I'd enjoy seeing my mother lowered in a six-foot-deep hole in the ground. I almost cried worrying about her. Jesus Christ. I was supposed to hate her for giving me to the monster and ignoring my existence for four long years. I wanted to hate her.

I struggled to fight off the nausea I always felt when trapped inside a shuddering, diesel-powered bus. Finally, sleep rescued me.

Dawn was breaking when Virginia and I staggered from the Greyhound bus in Evanston, Wyoming. Both of us used the station restroom. I finished much quicker than her and anxiously watched the door to the women's restroom. I needed to keep a close watch on my mother. Deep inside of me gnawed the fear that she might decide to take off alone. Once again, she'd leave me behind. I didn't trust her at all. I relaxed when she rejoined me.

We ate breakfast in a nearby café. I felt better as I wolfed down her generous purchase of fried eggs, ham, fried potatoes, toast, and a cup of coffee with lots of cream. She looked scary pale. She ate dry toast, drank black coffee, and smoked.

We each carried a suitcase as we walked out to the highway. We found a good hitching spot, and I stuck my thumb out, so she wouldn't have to. The day was cloudless, the bright sun warmed us, and traffic picked up. I was experiencing another new beginning to life. She stood next to me smoking a cigarette. It was just her and I against the world. A semi-truck horn blared and the driver waved to her. She ignored him. We weren't looking to bounce around in any rough riding, eighteen-wheelers crammed next to a stinking, long-haul driver.

"We're going to save precious money by hitchhiking rather than taking a bus to Saint Louis, Mickey. We should have good luck getting rides here on Route 30." She smiled reassuringly at me. Every sign of life from her lifted my spirits. I couldn't shake the thought of her taking deadly pills.

"Yeah, we should. How're you feeling?"

"I'm feeling much better, Mickey. Thank you."

I felt responsible for her physical well-being. I also felt responsible for whether or not she smiled. Keeping another person healthy and happy was a daunting task.

A newer sedan pulled over, carelessly spraying gravel. A too eager, balding, middle-aged man jumped out of the driver's side.

"Hi. I'm Phil." He flashed a big, phony salesman's smile at us. "Let me offer you a ride."

"Hello, Phil. I'm Virginia. This is my son, Mickey."

"It's really nice to meet both of you, Virginia and Mickey. I'm on my way to a funeral in Lincoln, Nebraska."

"I'm sorry about the funeral," she sympathized.

"Oh, that's okay."

"We're going to Saint Louis, Phil. Lincoln Nebraska will get us a long way to our destination."

"That'll be wonderful," he said. "I don't like to travel alone."

Phil shook my hand. His fat hand was cold and clammy.

With a clumsy flourish, he helped her with her suitcase and rushed to hold the front passenger door open for her. I lifted my suitcase up in the trunk. I slammed the lid shut and took my place in the backseat. Lincoln, Nebraska! This is going to be a long, comfortable ride. What good luck.

"How old are you, son?" He turned around to look at me and flashed another phony smile.

"I'm fifteen, sir."

We were quickly on the road. Phil drove at the speed limit and we burned away miles as he gabbed non-stop. My mom nodded her head as he droned on. I watched the boring western scrubland pass by. Only road signs broke the monotony of the lifeless landscape. Phil liked to recite the Burma Shave rhymes out loud.

"Hardly a driver
Is now alive
Who passed
On hills
At 75
Burma Shave."

That's a funny one," he chortled.

"Yes it is," my mom agreed.

I had to admit, I liked the silly word play Burma Shave erected along these desolate highways to entertain bored travelers.

We stopped at Little America, the famed and popular oasis of the Wyoming vastness. It was like a grand, although small, amusement park magically appeared over the rise of a hill. In the middle of nowhere, with no human habitation visible for miles, lots of entertainment was offered.

I studied the stuffed wildlife on display in the spacious, high-ceilinged and colorful lobby. Standing in a threatening pose was a massive Grizzly bear at least nine-feet-tall. His deadly teeth showed as he growled with great volume and his long, sharp claws were fully extended. A snow-white polar bear, also growling ferociously, appeared to be rushing at me for the kill. Heavily antlered moose, elk and deer were impressively beautiful creatures. A wolf with its hackles raised glared threateningly at me and a coyote slunk menacingly.

Displayed on the wall behind the long, heavy oak, old-west style bar in the saloon was a jackalope. The sign said a jackalope was a jackrabbit that grew antelope horns. It's a "fearsome critter" the words trumpeted. The creature certainly looked authentic, but I wasn't totally convinced.

Virginia and I enjoyed pie and coffee in the large restaurant which was crowded with noisy travelers. Upon our arrival at this wonderfully glitzy place, our new friend, Phil, immediately headed to the bar.

When we got back on the road, Phil carried three cans of beer. As we rolled east, he held the steering wheel with one hand, and clutched a can of beer with the other. He rapidly consumed his three beers and ended with a big burp.

"Excuse me, Virginia."

Whenever a saloon appeared along the highway, he pulled over and entered the cool darkness of the roadside drinking holes. Virginia and I waited in the car as he drank. She scowled and fumed.

"I'm really worried about his drinking and driving," she said. Her irritation was visibly growing.

"Should we look for another ride?" I asked.

"I'm thinking about it." Concern creased her face.

Phil wobbled back to the car and awkwardly slid in the driver's seat. He clumsily pulled back onto the road. Lurching crazily, he got us back up to speed. His erratic driving frightened both her and me. He nodded off and on as if he needed to take a long nap. The car wandered way too much on the narrow two-lane highway. Playing games with huge, long-haul trucks barreling along this asphalt was suicidal. The semi's passing us going in the opposite direction made Phil's car shimmy down to its tires. On many stretches the shoulder was only a couple of inches wide. With Phil's crazy driving, the tires drifted onto loose gravel far too often. There wasn't any room for error and Phil drove like a drunken fool. I was sure I'd die a horrible, bloody death when a towering semi-truck ripped our small vehicle into tiny shards of metal.

"Would you please be more careful, Phil," Virginia pleaded.

CHAPTER THIRTY-FOUR

Finally, Phil realized he was too drunk to drive. We stopped at a cheap motel next to a busy truck stop. He generously rented a room for Virginia and me and one for himself. She and I ate at the truck stop café. I was almost full after a hot-roast-beef plate, which was two slices of roast beef over a slice of white bread and mashed potatoes covered with gravy; one of my favorite meals.

In our small room, there were enough blankets for me to put together a comfortable pallet on the carpeted floor. She didn't offer to share her bed with me anymore. The memory of my sinful dreams, with her and me naked and snuggling under bedclothes, continued to horrify me. As we settled in our room, a loud knock sounded at the door.

"Who is it," Virginia yelled.

"It's me. It's Phil," he slurred through the closed door. "Come on, Virginia. Have a drink with me."

"No," she said. "You're very drunk, Phil. Go to your room and get some sleep."

"Oh, come on, Virginia. Please have a drink." He banged

more loudly with his fist and kicked our door. His kicking made the thin wood barrier rattle loosely in its frame. "I'm not going to give up, Virginia!"

"Help me push the dresser against the door, Mickey."

Working together, we pushed the heavy dresser over to block entry to our room. Phil still called for her. "Come on, Virginia. Have a little drink with me."

"Quit all the fucking noise!" an irate voice several rooms over shouted.

Phil gave up. The person yelling sounded like a burly, truck driver with big fists. I didn't think Phil was much of a fighter, no matter how drunk.

The next morning, Phil showed up as we ate breakfast. Pale-faced and shaky, he slid in my side of the booth. I inched away from him until my elbow bumped against the window overlooking the parking lot and busy gas pumps. His hands trembled and his eyes were painfully bloodshot. He struggled to open his bottle of aspirin.

"I'm really sorry about last night," he mumbled. He downed several of the white pills and took a gulp from the glass of water the waitress placed in front of him. "That wasn't like me at all. I drank too much."

"I can't tolerate drunken behavior," Virginia admonished him. "If you aren't going to act decently, Phil, we'll look for a ride with someone else."

"Oh," Phil mumbled through his cottonmouth. "I'll be a perfect gentleman from now on, Virginia."

I was sure he still hoped my mother would finally succumb to his charm.

. . .

Virginia now sat in the back seat with me. The biggest annoyance from being around her when she was unattached was men coming after her like dogs in heat. I hated that. I guess because she was out on the open-road hitchhiking, they thought she was easy.

Phil stayed away from booze and quit his nonstop chattering. The miles melted away. We arrived in Lincoln, Nebraska, where he deposited us at a good hitching spot.

"I sure would like to see you again, Virginia," he pleaded.

"Thanks a lot for the ride, Phil," she answered with finality.

I suspected he was far more depressed about missing a chance with her than about the funeral he was to attend.

"Good riddance to him," Virginia said as we watched his car disappear.

"That was some scary stuff," I said.

"We did cover a lot of miles." She put her hand on my shoulder. I saw it coming, so I didn't flinch from her touch; a big improvement on my part.

Virginia and I continued our trek from Ogden, Utah to Saint Louis, Missouri. I stepped out front and stuck out my thumb. Some drivers slowed down, looked us over, and then sped on. What the hell were they looking for?

A black, hot-rod coupe pulled over alongside us. The engine and muffler rumbled loudly. Rock and roll music blared from its radio. The guy in the passenger seat wore a black leather jacket studded with silver ornamentation. His greasy, dark hair was slicked back. His eyes looked unnaturally glassy. He slurred his greeting as he looked us over like we were lambs waiting to be slaughtered.

"Hey lady, we can take you a couple of hundred miles," he mumbled from his seat in the shuddering car.

Virginia hesitated. "Are you sure there's room in your car?"

"There's lots of room back there, lady," the driver shouted from his seat. He stared over his shoulder at us.

She relented. "Well, it sounds okay. This is my son, Mickey." The back seat of the jalopy didn't look big enough for a pair of skinny midgets.

The driver popped the trunk with an inside lever. We squeezed our suitcases in the small space. The short passenger slithered out of his seat. He pulled the seat forward for access to the rear. With a sloppy wave of his hand, he invited us to climb in the cramped back seat. He leered at her as she struggled to squeeze her way in. He reminded me of a rattle-snake ready to strike. It was easier for me to climb in. She and I were trapped.

The driver, who was sitting slouch-low in his seat, was attired similarly to Shorty. They both looked to be in their mid-twenties. Slouch, the driver, stared at us in the rear-view mirror. He gunned the engine and carelessly spun onto the pavement. Shorty turned sideways in his seat so he could look back at us. His face showed a crazy-in-the-head demeanor. His mouth was set in a sneer.

"You must be proud to have such a good-looking mama, kid." He looked from me to her.

I didn't answer the rude son-of-a-bitch.

The driver, Slouch, raced the engine and made quick starts and stops. "We're trying to get a fun party together, lady," he slurred over his shoulder.

"We have a funeral to attend in Saint Louis," Virginia lied. "We're really in a hurry."

As we noisily lurched down the town's main drag, the two hoods kept looking behind the car as if they were worried about something. I turned around.

"There's a police car right behind us, Mom." I never called

her "Mom," but the word forced its way out of me in this frightening situation.

"Aren't you worried about your noisy muffler, boys?" she yelled above the din.

"Naw, lady," mumbled Slouch.

"Sure you don't want to have a party, lady? We have lots of good booze," cajoled Shorty.

"No, I can't go to a party. My son and I need to keep traveling."

"Well, you're the boss, lady."

Slouch pulled off the road next to a gas station.

"Sorry we couldn't take you further, lady. We have to get to our party."

It took quite an effort to climb out of the cramped back seat. Shorty slouched with his ass against the front fender and looked disappointed we escaped his trap. He didn't come close to offering Virginia a hand. What a bum. Slouch did pop the trunk, but neither of the lazy louts offered any help in lifting our luggage out of the tiny trunk.

We walked a few yards and set our luggage down. The two hooligans roared away.

"Well," Virginia said. "Those guys were crazy."

"They sure were," I agreed. A promised two-hundred-mile ride turned to a short cruise down the main street of Lincoln, Nebraska with two slimy thugs. I was glad to get away from them with my life. The police car tailing us pulled over to the side of the road fifty-feet away, parked with the engine running, and the copper watched us. He waited until we got our next ride with a smiling, old couple that wanted to know the sad story of our lives. I really appreciated the cop keeping an eye on Virginia and I.

Virginia described our close call with the hoods to our new benefactors.

"The Lord was looking after you," the old lady said.

"Amen!" the old man added.

He drove at the speed of a snail, she talked without taking a breath, and traffic backed up behind us. Neither of them noticed the honk of horns as autos and semi's cranked up their engines to pass. Irate drivers shook their fists at us and visibly cursed.

After the slowest auto ride I ever experienced on an open highway, the good-hearted, but clueless old folks, dropped us off in Nebraska City.

"Remember to pray to the Lord," the old lady intoned.

"I always do." Virginia smiled. "Thank you so much for the ride."

We both waved goodbye as they putted away. A long, bumpy road remained ahead before we'd reach our destination of Saint Louis, Missouri. I believed we'd make it. Virginia was a seasoned survivor of these flights from the several husbands she'd grown disenchanted with.

CHAPTER THIRTY-FIVE

A Saint Louis city bus was our last mode of transport in Virginia's runaway from Al Davey.

It was dark when we finally arrived at Goldie's apartment building located in a mostly decrepit and often dangerous neighborhood. We reached our refuge and a raucous and loving welcome greeted us. Goldie's home was always open to her first and favorite child, Virginia. I couldn't imagine being the oldest of thirteen siblings. Dealing with four brothers was challenging enough for me.

Living with Goldie were Virginia's brother Ronnie, age twenty-three, half-brothers Randy and Jimmy, age twenty and sixteen, and Virginia's seven-year-old half-sister, Lela Darlene. I was intrigued by the idea of having a seven-year-old aunt.

I couldn't recall anything but mild indifference from my Grandmother Goldie. She always favored my oldest brother, dark-haired Tommy. She liked his manly ways and his enthusiastic greetings of her. By the time I was born, she had far too many children and grandchildren crowding around her to pay much attention to me. With my whitish-blond hair, I looked like a stray kid from the neighborhood. I didn't try to go through any of the phony "I love you, Grandma" hugs and kisses crap, because I was sure she'd look at me like I was crazy.

Goldie had dropped out of school after the fourth grade. She had confined her recreational reading to gossip magazines and the Bible. For years she labored on hands and knees as a scrubwoman, cared for her family, and attended nursing classes in her spare time. She eventually earned a nursing certificate and for the last twenty years worked as a practical nurse at the city insane asylum. The under-funded and despised institution was crowded with psychopathic rapists and murderers. Daily, she rode a city bus to her workplace, the St. Louis City Hospital #1 Malcom Bliss. On many nights during those years, on her way home from her house-of-horrors job, she stopped at a pub to drink several beers and normalize.

She had given birth to thirteen children with different husbands. When at home, she cleaned house and cooked. Rarely did she find any time to rest. When she sat down, a grateful sigh of exhaustion deflated her enlarged body. She lived in her small apartment for many years as the neighborhood declined around her. Rent control made it a bargain she couldn't abandon.

Foul smells embedded in the walls, ceilings, floors, and stairwells of her St. Louis slum building. The stench brought back memories of my early childhood in Chicago's north side industrial slums. When it was warm enough to open the windows in her small flat, the noise and stench of the surrounding neighborhood flowed into her cramped living quarters. With limited fresh air available inside or outside, I struggled to decide which was worse. I usually chose to seek relief on the back outside-stairway's small landing.

Virginia told me while he played the piano in saloons and low-class night clubs, her half-Cherokee father Harry nursed glasses of cheap whiskey and chain-smoked cigarettes he rolled by hand. Late one night, while playing a rowdy tune on the piano in a smoke-filled bar, he slumped over and his cigarette fell from his lips. A massive heart attack killed him at the age of fifty-five. Virginia had loved her father deeply. Never a financial success in life, Harry was nevertheless always a kind and gentle man. Virginia greatly admired her father for his character and his musical talent. His sudden and untimely death was extremely difficult for her.

Whenever Virginia talked about her father, she always said, "I adored him." When she mentioned her mother, she said, "Her home is always open to me as a refuge. I really love her."

I often wondered why members of my mother's family didn't open their arms, offer a home, and save me from four brutal years of abuse from Naomi in Chicago. Did my mother ask any of them for help before she decided to give me to the monster? Did her family say they didn't have room for me? Maybe they just didn't want me. I never worked up the courage to ask those questions. I decided on my own, I was just too different from everyone in my mother's and father's families. I wouldn't have been a good fit in any of their households. I knew my ignorant and cruel father hated me. He decided I was a bastard the first time he saw me. I knew most of his family viewed me the same way. No welcome for me existed among them. Being a giveaway child and a slave to Naomi was the best I could hope for. A nine-year-old unwanted boy wasn't welcome anywhere, except by those with evil intentions. In any case, I had adjusted to the fact I was on my own to survive in the world.

Goldie had remarried and had given birth to her daughter, Lela Darlene, when she was forty-six-years old.

Now, Lela followed Virginia around like a just-weaned puppy dog. Virginia happily returned her little sister's affection.

"Ginny, I love you." Lela chimed constantly as she climbed up onto Virginia's lap and wrapped herself around her oldest sister like a baby monkey clings to its mother, never wanting to let go.

Virginia took charge of the cooking and organizing in her mother's crazy household. Goldie sank in her softest chair where she drank beer, smoked cigarettes, and enjoyed the attention from her many children and grandchildren.

Virginia's younger brother Alfred visited. As a seven-year-old, my mother was a second mother to him when he was a baby and toddler and they still shared a great affection. Handsome and well-built, he liked to joke and tell stories. He made everyone around him smile and laugh. Like the movie stars Virginia admired so much, he had dark hair, smiled easily, and filled out his short-sleeve, muscle-man shirt and neatly pressed slacks to perfection. He was pleasant to me and I admired him and wished I was like him. At fifteen-years-old, I remained a moody, skinny introvert who was haunted by merciless demons. There wasn't any way I'd ever reach his level of reverence in my mother's affections.

Goldie's three younger sons, who still lived at home with her, had three cots crowded in one tiny eleven by twelve-foot room. That limited space was divided in three jealously guarded domains. While I sat on Randy's cot, Jimmy pretended to be asleep while he humped his bed. Ronnie and Randy ignored him. I tried to ignore him and really wanted to leave the room, but as usual, I succumbed to my habitual weakness of not wanting to offend anyone. Finally, Ronnie spoke up. "Quit,

Jimmy. We have company." Jimmy quit humping and feigned sleep.

As he sat on his cot and rummaged through his cache of candy he pulled from underneath his bed, Ronnie's hands and mind also became occupied with the widespread volcanic eruption of pimples on his face.

"I'd better find my Snickers bar or one of you is dead," he warned his two brothers.

"Well, maybe little Lela snuck in here and ate your precious candy, Ronnie!" Randy replied with a feigned pout.

"If she did, I'll smack her little ass."

Randy, I discovered, was in transition. He wore male clothing during the day, but dressed up in women's finery to go out at night. As darkness approached, he picked through his limited collection of female garments. He struggled to put together the perfect outfit. After a lot of work at his small mirror hung from a nail hammered in the plaster wall, he turned to me and smiled.

"Don't I look fabulous, Mickey? Now, you can call me Debi!"

His makeup created a shocking change in my uncle. The lipstick he'd liberally applied to his lips looked overdone to me.

"Looks nice, Randy," I replied, not wanting to offend.

"It's, Debi, Mickey. D. E. B. I.!"

His brothers ignored him.

CHAPTER THIRTY-SIX

The pleasure of the visit with my mother's family was interrupted when Al Davey tracked us down. He desperately wanted Virginia to return to him. The phone rang constantly with his calls, but she dramatically refused to talk to him. The tension grew thick in the household and made everyone irritable.

Finally, she took the receiver. "No. No. I don't love you, Al. I'm never coming back to Utah. Please leave me alone."

I heard his plaintive voice coming out of the phone. "Please let me come out there to see you, Virginia."

"I don't love you, Al."

"I'm desperate. I love you. I'll drive to Saint Louis and we can talk, Virginia. Please."

"No, Al. Never."

"Please, Virginia. I'm begging you!"

"Well, if you insist, you can drive to Saint Louis. But I'm not going to change my mind."

Why the hell did she agree to his visit?

. . .

Two days later, an exhausted and haggard Al Davey arrived in Saint Louis. Peggy wasn't with him, a big disappointment for me. Just like I saw in the stupid Hollywood movies, he got down on one knee in front of Virginia and pleaded with her to take him back. He swore he'd follow her to the ends of the earth. Anything she demanded of him, he'd obey. Just give him one more chance. He even bought a pitiful bouquet of flowers for her.

I watched the scene with excruciating embarrassment. Then, I remembered. When I was nine-years-old, I begged my mother with tears flowing not to leave me with the monster, Naomi. She ignored my pleading and walked away and abandoned me. Goddamn her to hell.

Exhausted by Al's groveling and overwrought entreaties, she finally relented. She insisted her seven-year-old half-sister, Lela, would join us for the drive back to Utah.

"It'll be a good vacation for her, Mom. She and I'll have the whole back seat of the car to ourselves. The men will sit up front. Lela and I'll have a wonderful time together."

I liked the idea of sitting up front in the car, but I didn't like being classified in the same weakling male category as Al. I was depressed by the thought of returning to Utah and the Mormons. I thought I had escaped that hell forever. I fantasized about Virginia and I hitchhiking north to Chicago and together, making our way in the world. A grand future awaited me.

If only I could find a way to survive on my own. But, how the hell would I house and feed myself and finish high school? Doing both at the same time seemed impossible for a fifteen-year-old boy who was afraid of interacting with people.

"I know you'll take wonderful care of Lela, Virginia," a

tearful Goldie lamented. "But, I'm going to miss my baby so much."

At that moment, I realized Lela would displace me and fill the vast void in Virginia's life. Hell. That was fine with me. I was my mother's physical and emotional support on her failed flight to freedom. I was weary of the responsibility. I didn't understand why I felt a sense of obligation to my mother at all when I always expected fickleness and betrayal from her.

We left Saint Louis and family warmth behind. Ahead lay the grueling drive back to Ogden, Utah. I wasn't happy about my forced future with Mormons, or the mostly boring sightseeing prospects along this recently traveled route.

In the backseat of the auto, Virginia had Lela to snuggle with and care for. When we stopped at a motel, they had a room to themselves. Al and I slept fitfully in the cramped space of the Pontiac.

During the relentlessly-dreary hours in the car, I appreciated Lela was along to fill the conversation void. Her little sister's voice and endless questions kept Virginia in a better mood. Lela's presence reduced the tension level between Virginia and Al to almost tolerable.

As the miles unrolled beneath us, Virginia happily pointed out the sights to Lela. She clearly enjoyed expanding her little sister's knowledge of the world. The only thing Al got from her was a cold shoulder and chilling contempt.

When we finally reached Ogden, I felt great relief the trip was over. I climbed out of the cigarette-smoke filled car. I knew in returning to Utah, I'd walked back through the gates of a religion-built prison. Nevertheless, the time in Saint Louis renewed my hope for an eventual total escape from this land of Mormon self-righteousness.

The attention Virginia showered on Lela during her visit in Ogden distracted her from heaping tons of constant punishment on poor Al Davey, but he still suffered mightily for being the greatest disappointment of her life.

A couple of months later, Uncle Ronnie rode the train from Saint Louis to Ogden for a short visit. He came to fetch Lela for the trip back to Saint Louis. Virginia celebrated her brother's visit, but she shed many tears over the departure of her little sister.

With the departure of Lela, the task of filling the great void in Virginia's life fell once again to Peggy. The chance I'd ever again fill that emptiness in my mother was remote. Surely, she realized during our flight to St Louis, I was only half-heartedly there for her. I never addressed her warmly with the precious word she loved to hear, Mom. My constant, tortuous, unfulfilled hope she'd return to North Hamlin Avenue and rescue me from my slavery to Naomi completely burned to ashes any trust I ever had in my fickle mother. Once again, a great distance existed between her and me.

CHAPTER THIRTY-SEVEN

Despite how pretty and pleasant she was, my stepsister Peggy didn't receive any respect from the Mormons. She wouldn't ever be forgiven for being a Salvationist rather than a disciple of Joseph Smith. Although she wasn't as hated as me, she still lived her life among the Latter-Day Saints as a friendless outcast.

Peggy and I both attended Ogden High School. One day, when I descended the rear stairwell and stopped between the second and third floor, I looked out the window overlooking the rear parking lot. I saw Peggy. She was hugging and kissing her Mexican boyfriend.

I already knew about Mario. I knew she was in love with him. She pressed her mouth and her body against a taller, more muscular, and more handsome male than I was or could ever hope to be. I worshipped her and she acted as if my love was nothing. The jagged pain of her rejection ripped through me and poisonous jealousy infected me.

I sank to the repulsive role of a lousy, low-life fink. I reported what I witnessed to Virginia.

My mother was scandalized. She told Peggy she couldn't have a Mexican boyfriend. She insisted there wasn't any future with a poor Mexican. Al Davey, finally speaking up strongly, agreed. Peggy condemned their prejudice. She declared her undying love for Mario. She shed a flood of tears while she gave me a killing look of hatred and contempt. She retreated to her room and slammed the door shut behind her.

I accompanied Al and Virginia when they paid a visit to Mario's family. With the windows rolled down and as I cowered in the back seat of the car, I spied upon and listened to the drama that unfolded.

The Gonzalez family lived in the poorest Mexican section of Ogden. They were a handsome and neat family, with three children younger than Mario. Their dilapidated, rented property had a bare dirt yard and their tin-roofed, patchwork-sided house looked more suitable for a flock of chickens than six humans.

I overheard them agree a relationship between a white girl like Peggy and their son wasn't appropriate. Despite the concession, these people, who wore traditional Mexican garb, appeared to maintain their dignity and pride. Maybe, the real truth was, they didn't want their Mexican son involved with a poor, white girl.

"Mario will obey me," the father said when he shook hands with Al Davey and Virginia. He labored valiantly to speak his best version of English. "You need not worry about your daughter."

An agreement was reached.

Although I despised myself for being a stinking rat, I relished the breakup of her romance with Mario.

. . .

Back at school, as I feared, I ran into Mario and his friends. Scorn and threats of violence radiated from their expressions and mutterings as they surrounded me. I was a flea-infested mouse cornered by a pack of snarling wolves. The tone of the angry words in Spanish convinced me they intended to kill me.

"Leave the little scum alone," Mario said in English. "It'd just be more trouble for me if we hurt him."

Peggy barely talked to me before, and now she refused to acknowledge my existence at all. Her relationship with Virginia was badly damaged. She was unusually aloof from her father. She crawled in a shell and I feared I wouldn't ever find the tiniest entry into her world.

It was 1957 and the country had plummeted into a serious recession. Continuing an ongoing trend, people quit using passenger trains. Layoffs in the railroad industry finally reached Al. He lost his beloved job at the Union Pacific. After 22 years of employment, he received two weeks of severance pay. Because of his low-level job status, the company didn't owe him one penny more. Many of his co-workers faced the same fate. There wasn't any work available for the sudden surge of jobless men in Ogden, Utah.

"You might find a job if you were related to Brigham Young or the Prophet Joseph Smith," a bitter voice complained.

The most vital part of Al's life was ruthlessly ripped away from him. He was totally devastated; a broken man. Judging by the way she looked at him, it appeared Al had sunk to an unimaginable new low in Virginia's estimation.

I sensed road-fever smoldering in my mother. The birth of every new spring infected her with an overpowering desire to be on the move. Like an octopus gripped its prey, wanderlust grabbed her with an unyielding hold. Like a bottle of sweet, red wine brings a glow to the eyes of a skid row drunk, the new buds of spring made her eyes sparkle with hope. She was certain the future offered a treasure of gold and diamonds if she just traveled down the next highway. Love and happiness always laid over the next hill. Nothing could keep her from surrendering to her feverish vision. I needed to watch her closely while her mind was in such turmoil. She could easily decide to take off in the middle of the night and leave me behind with an emotionally-crippled Al Davey.

I was shaken awake from a deep sleep. I forced my eyes open. I was surrounded by semi-darkness.

I focused on Al Davey hovering over me. "Wake up, Mickey. I need to talk to you."

Reluctantly, I sat up.

"Virginia's gone. She left us."

"My mother's gone?"

"Yes. I woke up and she wasn't there."

"Are you sure she's gone?"

"I looked everywhere. Her suitcase and all her personal belongings are gone."

I struggled to full alertness. His words hit me like a punch to my stomach. Goddamn my mother. She took to the road and left me behind. She abandoned me again.

"I just don't understand her," Al lamented through his tears. "I tried to do everything for her."

Understand her? Why the hell did he think he should be able to understand her?

"What am I supposed to do, Mickey?" His eyes were already red from crying.

I didn't have any answers for him. I liked Al, but I was uncomfortable with his weakness around my mother. I certainly wouldn't cry in front of people the way he did. I did my best to hide my feelings of grief. Why couldn't he?

"I really love her," he said.

To love Virginia was a fatal curse for a man like Al Davey. My reservoir of pity for him and his stupid love was running dry. I had plenty of my own problems in dealing with her.

I quit trusting Virginia long ago. The brutal truth was I had quit loving her long ago, but I didn't have anyone else to live with. There wasn't anyone else in the world obligated to offer me shelter. It didn't matter how reluctantly the shelter was offered, even I needed help sometimes.

I used many tricks to get my mother's attention without using the word I hated to say, "Mom." That meaningless word always stuck in my throat.

I never said, "I love you." with any sincerity to her. If forced to, I muttered the lie as indecipherably as possible. She easily and often said, "I love you." to me. Her tone and her look demanded I repeat the falsehood back to her. Sometimes, I mumbled the meaningless words when she looked at me with threatening expectation. Most of the time, I flat out refused to voice the lie even though I feared angry rejection from her.

After much searching, shedding more tears than I ever wanted to see, and asking me a thousand questions about human relationships I couldn't answer, Al located Virginia in Chicago.

"I telephoned her. She told me to stay in Ogden. She said she didn't want anything to do with me anymore. She said she wants a divorce," Al gripped a cup of coffee and a Pall Mall cigarette as he painfully recited her brutal words.

"She didn't ask to talk to me?"

"No, she didn't, Mickey. I'm sorry."

I wanted to scream in her face, "why the fuck did you leave me behind?" Of course, I wouldn't ever have the courage to confront her to her face.

Before Al lost his railroad job, he'd bought a slightly used 1955 Ford sedan. He loved his two-tone-blue, four-door automobile. Now, without any income and debts piling up, he didn't know how he'd finish paying for his rakishly-styled vehicle. He was horrified by the thought of losing it. He'd already lost most everything of value in his life.

"Come with me, Mickey. We'll drive to Chicago and I'll talk to her."

"Do you think that'll help?"

"I'm sure it will, Mickey. If only I can talk to her."

"That's a long drive, Al. But, if you want me to, I'll go with you."

"Thanks, Mickey."

I was always ready for a road trip. I longed for an escape from Utah and the Mormons. And, this was Chicago we'd be traveling to. Chicago was the city where I was born and grew up. Chicago was also where I was enslaved and imprisoned by the monster, Naomi. But, the brutal prison-warden was dead and buried deep in a cold, dark hole. I wouldn't ever again let myself be locked away into solitude. Hopefully, I wouldn't ever have to return to Utah, my Latter-Day Saints hell.

Peggy refused to accompany us. We didn't know how this venture would turn out and she wasn't in the mood to spend time on the road, in a cigarette-smoke filled car, with either of us.

Al and I loaded some of our personal possessions in the car and started out on what certainly appeared to be a hopeless mission.

CHAPTER THIRTY-EIGHT

I hadn't driven a car before and didn't have a driver's license. The Ford had a manual transmission, so between the numerous small towns, Al coached me through the shifting process until I got up to speed. After much grinding, lurching, and stalling, I reached third gear and quickly developed a feel for guiding the car along the narrow two-lane highways.

I worked up to a speed of sixty-five miles an hour and successfully navigated the suction created by big semis going in the opposite direction. Those behemoths roared threateningly close, only a few feet from my elbow resting on the open driver's window and they threw us momentarily into their mountainous shadow. A big challenge for me was my first time passing a double-trailer semi.

A large eighteen-wheeler loomed menacingly in the narrow lane in front of us. I managed to see around him and a clear road ahead. As I pulled in the other direction lane, I pushed the gas pedal all the way down. The Ford surged forward. We broke clear of the towering truck's draft. Now next to us, its huge tires thumped noisily on the roadway. We caught up to the tall cab and the driver smiled down at us. When I was far enough ahead of him, the trucker gave me an all-clear signal with his horn. I pulled triumphantly back in the lane and gave him a thank you wave. I now knew I'd be a good open road driver.

During one long, arrow-straight downgrade crossing Wyoming, I pushed the gas pedal to the floor and held it there. The eight-cylinder engine surged with power and the Ford leapt forward. I hoped all the bolts holding the two-hundred-horse power-plant to the chassis were strong.

At 80-miles-per-hour the car shuddered. At one-hundred-miles-per-hour the engine whined. I gripped the steering wheel so tightly, my knuckles turned white. The speedometer needle bounced off the maximum one-hundred-twenty miles per hour peg. Vibrations coursed through the car. Al stirred from his nap. Sleepy-eyed, he looked over at the speedometer. He glanced at me. Wordless, he looked at the clear road ahead of us. He repositioned his head against his seat and closed his eyes. Quickly, he was back to sleep. As we approached the end of the downgrade, I reluctantly eased up on the gas pedal. We decelerated to a snail's pace of sixty-five miles per hour.

Traveling through a hot, humid Iowa night, millions of insects pelted us. It was like the dirty-white snow of a brutal Chicago winter blizzard. In order for us to see the road ahead, we stopped at gas stations every hour or so just to clean the thousands of splattered victims from our windshield and headlights. Large and small bloody splotches from moths, crickets, and fireflies covered the front of the car. Some bugs I never saw the likes of before were slaughtered by our forward surge. An occasional bird became embedded in the grille. Fortunately, the jack rabbits and other small varmints we collided with, bounced off the front of the car, instantly dead or to die along the side of the road. I didn't want to see those victims up close. At some stops, we needed to hose away a dense, bloody mess from the front of the radiator so the engine could breathe. I marveled at the billions of bugs that survived and still filled the night like a snowstorm.

Bleary eyed farm boys wore oil company uniforms as they worked their attendant's job at shiny-new gas emporiums. Under the fluorescent-glow of the bright lights, alien-green, pimpled faces reacted sullenly to our arrival. They stared at us with cow-like expressions as they shoved the gas nozzle in the filler neck. My oldest brother, Tommy, once informed me they stuck their dicks in farm girls with the same finesse. I wanted, but failed to picture that scene clearly.

"Would'ya like the oil checked, sir?"

"No, thanks," a wary Al always answered. "I'll check it myself." He learned long ago not to trust any gas station oil checks. Some quoted false readings of the dipstick and tried to sell you other people's overused, recently-drained oil.

Back on the road, I blinked my weary eyes in the blinding brightness of oncoming headlights. Too many road-dazed drivers didn't bother or remember to dim their lights.

"You goddamn asshole," I cursed and felt better.

CHAPTER THIRTY-NINE

The first sight of Chicago brought a flood of mixed emotions to me. I experienced some good and endured lots of evil in the city, but it was the only place I ever felt at home.

Al struggled to follow the directions Virginia impatiently recited to him over the phone. We helplessly wandered the maze of Chicago's busy streets. Finally, we found her building.

"This is it." Al sounded like a man who was attending his own execution. I also feared the reception I'd get from her. Once again, she walked away and left me behind. This latest betrayal by her brought many bad memories back to haunt me. I couldn't wrap my mind around any answers to the question that nagged at me. What is my defect that makes it so easy for her to walk away, leave me behind, and forget my existence?

Virginia informed Al she managed an apartment building on the north side in Uptown Chicago. She opened the door to the exhausted and grimy pair of us. She gave me a welcoming smile and hugged me. She gave him a homicidal stare that would've made a fearless burglar turn and run for his life.

Al pleaded with her. He begged. He declared his never-ending love. She showed absolutely no sincere sympathy to him. But, once again she was exhausted by his pleas. She relented. She threw him a lifeline.

"If you want to move to Chicago, Al, you'll probably have a better chance of finding work here than back in Utah. You'll have to drive back to Ogden to get Peggy and whatever possessions you want to move."

"I can do that, Virginia," he said. His voice was meek, but his entire demeanor was picked up by this tiny glimmer of hope.

"I'm not promising you anything, Al. When you return, we can talk about our marriage. I really don't see any hope of saving it. I just don't want to be married to you anymore. I do worry about Peggy's future though."

Goddamn her. She worried about Peggy's future. Jesus Christ. She never worried about my future.

"There are a few of my things I'd like you to bring for me, Al," she said.

She and I didn't talk about her leaving me behind when she left Ogden. As in the past, we pretended her betrayals and abandonment of me never happened.

Buoyed by false hopes, Al set out on his long journey from Chicago to Ogden, Utah and back to Chicago. Damn. A lot of miles ground away on boring roads. I wished him the best.

I was excited about him bringing Peggy to Chicago. I was a veteran of the city and surely that would impress her and she'd need my guidance.

. . .

The area of northern Chicago where Virginia now lived was much cleaner and safer than the neighborhoods of my Chicago childhood. It was a pleasant, early-summer day as I walked the nearby streets on my job search. I asked for work at every business which showed promise. I loved being back in a society where my lack of membership in the Mormon Church didn't limit my employment opportunities. Chicago people reacted to me like I was just another city boy looking for a summer job.

I quickly found bona-fide employment.

My new job was at the Aragon Food Market located directly across the street from the palatial Aragon Ballroom on Lawrence Avenue. They hired me to be a full-time bagger, shelf stocker, and delivery boy at a wage of seventy-five-cents an hour. They didn't ask about my religion or require that I believed in the phony prophet, Joseph Smith. I struck gold.

"We need your social security number, Mickey."

I handed them my newly acquired Social Security card. Although they wrote down my real and official name "Robert Michael," I didn't feel like adjusting to the Robert moniker.

"I always go by Mickey," I told them.

I decided to be "Mickey" to any new Chicago friends. It was less complicated. Everyone in my family knew me by and addressed me as "Mickey." Officially, on paperwork, I would be the other person, "Robert." Living with two different names didn't seem like it would be a problem. I was used to instantaneous transformation.

Another boy my age worked at the store. Paul was as scrawny as I was and we hit it off immediately.

I rapidly learned the ins-and-outs of my new profession. As with any work I did, I was totally focused on being good at it.

A fun part of my great position at the market was making

weekly deliveries across the street to the bar at the Aragon Ballroom. The luxurious interior of the Chicago landmark resembled a Moorish castle. I wasn't old enough to attend the live big-band dances or buy cocktails for the party girls who crowded the immense dance floor on weekend nights, but I liked wandering the cavernous interior during my deliveries. The high ceiling was painted to resemble a deep-blue, starry Spanish sky. Thick gold paint glowed on many surfaces. Middle Eastern and Aztec murals decorated the walls. Giant swords protruded from above the wide stage. An extravagant grand staircase led to the second level.

Another perk of my new grocery-store job was a free lunch. Paul and I both had sandwiches from the deli meat section, along with a bag of chips, a quart of chocolate milk, and a package of twin Hostess cupcakes. As a challenge and running joke, the deli workers made our sandwiches larger and larger by piling on more ingredients.

One fat butcher commented, "Jesus Christ. How can two scrawny fifteen-year-olds eat so much?" I readily and easily accepted the challenge.

I delivered orders of groceries throughout the neighborhood. The toughest part was to carry two full grocery bags up four or five flights of stairs to studio apartments of elderly people. Most of the old, four and five story buildings didn't have elevators and charged a lower rent for walkups. Many oldsters found it difficult to climb the steps just to get to their home. They couldn't handle the extra burden of purchases from a shopping trip. Some old folks called their grocery orders in to the store on a shared, hallway telephone. Lonely seniors were stranded on the higher floors and navigated the many, steep stairs only when absolutely necessary.

Sometimes the aged customers gave me a nickel tip. Others acted like a couple of pennies were a fortune. One old woman always grouched at me for carrying her bags of groceries too tight and crushing everything inside. I showed her all the contents were perfectly fine. She still grumbled, but I didn't mind. I really liked this job and the freedom of living in Chicago.

Paul owned a Vespa motor scooter. His small, two-wheeled vehicle became the mode of transportation for the two of us when we were together. We zipped around the city on it, our combined weight badly overloading the scooter's flimsy shock absorbers. He never let me drive, so I always sat on the hard and narrow passenger seat. I felt the full impact of every bump we encountered, especially when we crossed streetcar tracks.

Like me, Paul enjoyed fishing. We ventured out onto and dangled our bamboo poles from the same Navy Pier where I spent many days of my childhood with my two older brothers. Some of our gear was more elaborate than what I used when I was a little kid, but the fun of being out on the pier and catching fish hadn't diminished one bit.

Paul picked me up at four in the morning in front of my apartment building. Loaded down with our fishing gear and lunches, the two of us tortured his poor little scooter and ourselves on the mostly empty, bumpy pre-dawn streets of Chicago. We were far out on the Navy Pier with our fishing gear set up as the sun rose over Lake Michigan. The air was cleaner, the smells more palatable, and the sky bluer on those cold, but glorious mornings. Dozens of seagulls serenaded us with their raucous symphony.

CHAPTER FORTY

After Al and unhappy Peggy arrived in Chicago, it took a lot of searching for Al to find a job in a warehouse as a common laborer. He hated his new job and living in the always bustling city of Chicago. The change was too drastic for a man whose greatest dream was retirement to simple farm life in a rustic house with a small flock of chickens. He needed to live, however poorly, in the spacious west of America.

When Paul saw Peggy, he immediately fell in love. She ignored him. She was not interested in a scrawny, blond fifteen-year-old. I still adored her, but finally realized my love would never be returned. I abandoned any hope she would recognize me as her Prince Charming, but her presence continued to torture me. Her breasts were getting bigger, her hips a bit wider, and her butt more prominent. I remained completely frustrated I couldn't picture what her totally naked body looked like.

Many other girls were in Chicago, especially the Catholic girls in their short uniform skirts crowding the elevated trains and buses to drive me crazy. I fantasized over and visualized them when I masturbated. I still hoped to eventually experience the wonderful sensation of putting my penis in a real, human female vagina. Please, I prayed to fate. Let it happen at least once before I die.

Peggy adjusted to life in Chicago much better than her father. She sat in our basement-level apartment and watched *American Bandstand* every afternoon on our small black and white television. Paul always wanted to hang around and watch her watch television.

"She's ripe, Mickey," he assured me. "I just need time to work on her. This is one of the best chances I'll ever have."

"Shouldn't you be at home doing your homework, Paul?" she teased him. She appeared to enjoy torturing him, but her attention always returned to the television and Dick Clark's Rock and Roll dance program broadcast live from Philadelphia. She focused on the guest stars, dance moves, clothing styles, and how intimate the dancer's bodies dared to be.

Her disgust for both of us grew more obvious when Frankie Avalon appeared on the show. She swooned over her dark and handsome Rock and Roll idol. To her eyes, Paul and I completely disappeared. Paul was a painfully slow learner, but I finally convinced him we could do better things with our time, like cruising the city on his scooter and fishing from the Navy pier.

I sat alone on the front steps of the walkway to our apartment building. A glassy eyed, nervous guy in his late twenties or early thirties, wearing khaki trousers and a light blue polo shirt, walked along the sidewalk. He eyed me as he approached and then he stopped in front of me.

"Hey kid," he blurted out as he looked down at me. "I'll give you twenty dollars if you let me suck your cock."

"Get the fuck out of here," I said as I stood and clenched my hands in fists.

Guilt and fear showed on his feverish face. He turned away from me and rapidly scooted away.

This wasn't the first time I was approached directly for sex and I was sure it wouldn't be the last. Now, I was a taller, quick-to-anger fifteen-years-old and could easily defend myself against most predators. Memories of when I was a frightened twelve-year-old, wandering the streets of Chicago by myself, still haunted me. For some reason, I seemed to be a target for the predators. They were relentless in their pursuit. There hadn't been much of a problem with this type of men in Ogden, Utah, but Chicago was overrun with them. Men who wanted to put their hands on my body and touch me. Men who wanted to suck young boy's cocks. Men who wanted to fuck young boys up the asshole. I wasn't absolutely sure how a person defined these creeps.

Most places I went by myself, the ghouls were a constant hassle. I guessed it was the price of being a young boy who spent too much of his time on the streets alone. Other guys my age talked about having the same problem. Nasty pansy and faggot jokes circulated freely. Those slurs were thrown about with abandon from boy to boy. Although careless insults of being a queer were tossed frequently, the fires of hell would've been more comfortable than the life of a young male seriously accused of being homosexual.

On a warm summer evening, Paul and I went to Riverview amusement park. I hadn't been to the fun place since I was eight-years-old and roamed the streets of Chicago with my two older brothers, Tommy and Ben. In those long ago days, my brothers and I loved the Water Bug, which was like the Dodge-ems, but on water. A kid could get really wet.

The Wild Mouse was the big roller-coaster attraction this year. I wasn't crazy about roller-coasters and really didn't like being stuck at the top of a Ferris wheel, but I did like the raucous mechanical and musical sounds of the tilt-a-whirl and even the merry-go-round. Once again, the freak show fascinated me the most. I did feel somewhat guilty about staring at the malformed oddities of nature. Fortunately, few of the freaks looked back at you directly. They were there physically, but many weren't there mentally.

The calliope music, smell of cotton candy, taste of corn dogs, and bright flashing lights, helped me fully enjoy being back in one of my favorite fantasy worlds. High school jocks wore team jackets and blonde cheerleaders, who wore brightly-colored team-sweaters, clung to their well-muscled arms. Black-leather jacketed toughs strolled jauntily, puffed deeply on cigarettes, and offered their arms to slutty girls wearing lots of makeup and sporting stacked hair. Many of the gum-smacking tough-girls hugged large stuffed animals won at games of skill by their cocky escorts. Soldiers and sailors with pints of whisky in their back pockets staggered about and tried to pick up the leftover girls.

This was my best summer ever and I believed the rest of my life was sure to improve. I was free of the Mormons. I freed myself from all aspects of religion and didn't fear hell anymore. No longer was I terrified of a vengeful god who was supposed to be living somewhere up in the sky.

CHAPTER FORTY-ONE

Consumed by curiosity but filled with foreboding, I rode a screeching, clattering elevated train to the neighborhood where I was enslaved for four years by Naomi Johnson. The sight of Garfield Park brought scenes back to my memory I hadn't wanted to recall. I remembered the sexual predators wandering the green oasis and loitering in the public toilets hunting for vulnerable young boys. I descended the steps from the station to the street. I walked down painfully familiar Hamlin Avenue. This was where the bullies taunted me, ran me down, and beat me. I sighted the house where I spent age nine through twelve in slavery and isolation. There was the terrible place where the beast, Naomi brutalized me. Rage surged through my body. Sour bile bubbled up in my throat. I wanted to strike out everywhere and at everyone with a killing weapon. Why the hell did I return to this shame-filled reminder of my childhood years of helplessness?

I spotted Margaret, the neighbor who had suffered from the effects of childhood polio. She was working in her garden close to the sidewalk. The demon inside me shriveled up and scurried back to his hiding place. I stopped next to Margaret's bent-over form. My shadow covered her and the patch of soil she worked. Appearing irritated, she looked up.

"Hello?"

"Hi, Margaret. I'm Mickey. I was the kid who lived next door with Naomi."

Her face brightened with recognition. "Oh, yes. Hi, Mickey," she smiled. "You've changed a lot. You're so tall. You're a young man."

"Thanks. Your garden looks really good."

"It's been a good year for the plants."

"How're you doing?"

"I'm doing well, Mickey."

She picked up her crutch, which lay next to her. She rearranged her leg brace and struggled to stand.

I pointed to my former prison. "What's happened there?" The second floor window I spent so many hours gazing out of, longing for the return of my mother and praying for my freedom from Naomi, showed heavy drapes closed to darken the interior. Naomi's voice echoed through my memory, "Where are you, Mickey, you monster? What are you doing, stupid?" I felt the impact of her fist against my face. A smeary blaze of fireworks filled my vision.

Margaret's voice interrupted my horrific recall.

"Emil married the white-trash he took up with when you still lived here. He sold the place and moved down south to live with her and her brood of bums."

"Really?"

"He got what he wanted. She got what she wanted."

"She didn't like me at all."

"She wanted you out of her way, Mickey."

Margaret and I talked a bit more about her garden and her life.

"My mother passed on," she lamented. "I really miss her. She's with God now. Someday, I'll be with her again."

CHAPTER FORTY-TWO

This was my sophomore year in high school and fall had arrived quicker than I wanted. I registered at Lane Technical High School, which Paul attended. A four-story, red-brick fortress with a twelve-story clock tower dominating its center, the boy-only institution was populated by four thousand pimple-faced, foul-mouthed, juvenile males. I really missed the scent and softness of girls in the classroom. Despite my many failures in dealing with the opposite sex, young female presence made the world a gentler, more pleasant place to live. I hoped someday I wouldn't be so frightened of them.

A group of us unpopular boys gathered at a coffee shop across the street from the campus. We smoked cigarettes, drank coffee, and talked filthy about girls. I listened to the rank conversations about females, but I didn't add to them unless I was directly challenged to prove my masculinity. Only then would I half-heartedly crawl down in the gutter to show I was one of the guys. I hated the words "cunt and tits" thrown around so freely.

Lane Tech was a good school. If you were scrawny like Paul and me, you knew the rules of survival. You stayed clear of the blustery jocks and hardcore hoods. Let them have the space they wanted. Sometimes, I would encounter somebody weaker than myself I could intimidate and move out of my way.

One month after the start of school, the challenge of managing the apartment building grew too overwhelming for Virginia. The danger posed by a belligerent tenant intimidated her and she feared for her safety. She always gave each of the two coppers a five-dollar tip when she called to report a problem and they showed up. They raised the tip/payoff to ten-dollars each and she couldn't afford that much. She gave up the job she mostly liked. We lost the free basement apartment that came with her manager's position.

Al was laid off from the menial job he hated. Peggy and I attended school full time and I only worked part time. The income required to support four people was non-existent. Virginia was having problems with her back and didn't want to go back to work as a waitress.

Virginia and Al hadn't reconciled. Why she finally agreed to return to Utah with him and leave Chicago behind was a total mystery to me. I wanted to stay in Chicago. I was willing to quit school and go to work fulltime. I was ready to find my own way in the world. I bought a black, leather jacket and pair of black, leather engineer boots and looked like a tough guy. A happy, big-city boy again, I knew how to dodge danger. I imagined if Virginia and I stayed in Chicago and she and I made the effort to survive as a mother and son team, I'd be perfectly satisfied with life.

Al hated Chicago and couldn't wait to leave and return to the familiar western part of America where he lived all his life.

Peggy didn't seem to really care which way things went. I was the only one who was doing well and wanted to stay in the big city. I dreaded a return to Utah and the scorn of the Latter-day Saints.

"I need you, Mickey," Virginia pleaded. "Please come back to Ogden with us. Don't abandon me."

I couldn't believe the words coming out of the mouth of the crazy woman who gave birth to me. But I lamented.

We set out on our return to hellish Utah. Despite the grind of the long drive, I enjoyed the gift of spending time in the back seat of the car with Peggy. I watched her facial expressions as she dreamed about her possible Prince Charming who was waiting in the wings to gallantly sweep her off her feet.

Back in Ogden, I was once again sleeping on a cot in a rented-house hallway. Every day, I attended a school and lived in a community where I was a despised, religious outcast.

It didn't take long for Virginia to find a saleslady job at a woman's dress shop in downtown Ogden. Al couldn't find any kind of employment. He drove her to work every morning and picked her up at the end of her shift. He worked sincerely at being a house husband, but was lousy at the job.

With my mother's recommendation and urging, I was hired by the dress shop as a box boy. It was the kind of job usually reserved for good Mormon boys and I wasn't well received by everyone. I assembled and ran boxes up from the basement and carried mannequins from their basement storage area up to the display windows in the front of the store. The saleswomen didn't like it if a box boy carried the mannequins with his hands touching the breasts, crotch or buttocks, or by hugging the fake body close to his filthy, horny body. Those perfectly proportioned female forms were made of thin plaster and weren't terribly heavy, but their realistic body size made them difficult to maneuver. When I struggled up the stairs from the basement with them and nobody was watching, I took liberties with their breasts and crotches. On the sales floor and in sight of the sales women, I was extremely careful. That gauntlet of glaring females scared the hell out of me.

It was also my job to clean the mannequins of any dust or grime accumulated in storage. When I washed number twenty-six, I fell in love with her. She had a complete torso and her arms were adjustable. I couldn't resist her loving smile. I made her wrap her arms around me and I kissed her on her mouth. Despite the painted on lipstick, she tasted like plaster.

Humping a mannequin was less than totally satisfying, but with a lot of imagination, I heard her say how much she loved me. To find any kind of privacy for masturbation was a real challenge, so when I worked alone in that basement surrounded by those lovely, firm, female nudes, I found myself in a painful paradise.

I came to work one day and saw number twenty-six standing in the front window. She wore a lovely summer frock, a sunbonnet, and glowed with vitality. Goddamn. There was only one way she got there. My crude, pimple-faced coworker carried her up the stairs in his fat, hairy arms. He'd put his greasy hands all over her perfect body. I was heartbroken.

My return to "no-welcome to non-Mormons" Utah meant I was back to attending Ogden High School. I showed up for my first class wearing my black leather jacket and black engineer boots I bought during my idyllic summer in Chicago.

"You think you're tough because you went to Chicago and bought a leather jacket," Mark the football player taunted. He bumped me with his heavily-muscled chest. "Well, I can kick your punk ass anytime, Shafer."

"I'm sure you can." I turned and walked away. He only outweighed me by fifty pounds and I knew when to dodge and run. I didn't want to have my handsome face smashed to a bloody pulp by some illiterate ape.

CHAPTER FORTY-THREE

Mark wouldn't let up on me. Whenever we crossed paths, he bumped me and delivered a quick, hard punch to my ribs.

"Fuck it," I said. "I'll meet you, Mark."

We did meet. Five of Mark's football friends showed up to cheer him. Nobody showed up to cheer me. Befitting my level of popularity among the powerful and privileged of Ogden High School, I was totally on my own. At this stage of my life, I never considered asking anybody for help or sympathy anyway. I didn't trust anyone.

Mark wore black football player gloves to protect his knuckles. I knew I was in big trouble. Mark approached me like I, as a young child, approached tiny ants attempting to cross a sidewalk. I cruelly crushed those innocent insects beneath my shoes. Retribution now strode my way.

Mark threw the first punch and his massive fist hit me squarely on my nose. I felt bone and cartilage give way. Blood spurted outward in a large spray. I would have gone down for good with that punch, but one of Mark's friends circling us, caught me and gleefully pushed me back in the fight.

Mark's gigantic fist sped towards my face again. Both of my lips split against my teeth. As I staggered backwards, I swallowed a large gob of blood and a couple of my front teeth. Another of Mark's ecstatic friends caught me and pushed me back in the fight.

I recalled my horrifying tour of the slaughter house in Chicago. I remembered the sight and sound of the sledge hammer striking the brown-eyed cows smack in the middle of their foreheads. I remembered their furry, brown and white bodies collapsing to the blood-soaked concrete floor.

Mark's sledgehammer fist flew at my face and connected to my left eye. The impact split my skin and crushed my eye socket. Blood flowed quick and heavy and I couldn't see out of that my eye anymore. Helpful hands caught me, kept me on my feet, and shoved me forward. Deep male voices cheered and screamed for more damage to my hated visage.

"Hit him again, Mark!"

Mark rammed his angry fist in my ribcage. I heard a loud crack. It sounded just like when I, as a young child, cruelly stomped on a fallen bird egg and killed the baby chick inside. Intense pain caused me to buckle at my waist and convinced me Mark broke several of my ribs. I couldn't breathe.

I fell down and curled in a ball. My beloved leather jacket was splotched with my blood. Someone gave me a solid kick to my spine that straightened me up momentarily. After I recovered from that hate-inspired blow, I curled in an even tighter ball, like the sow bugs I, as a young child, gleefully crushed with the tip of a sharp stick. My beloved black leather engineer boots didn't help me stay on my feet. My tough guy wardrobe didn't make me very tough.

"Get up, you pansy," a faraway voice yelled. Loud bells

pealed in my head and bright fireworks exploded across the inside of my eyelids.

I laid motionless and silent on the ground. I played dead.

"We took care of that faggot!"

I heard a spitting sound. A gob of mucus landed on my cheek. I didn't dare move to wipe that filthy moisture away.

I listened to Mark and his friends laugh as they strolled away.

After I was sure everyone was gone and I was alone and unobserved, I struggled to my feet. Like a skid row drunk, I careened homeward. I drug myself in the silent house. Thankfully, nobody was there. I didn't look in the mirror. I wanted to always remember my face as being pretty and pure. I swallowed a handful of aspirin and downed a gulp of water. I wrapped my sleeping bag around my aching body and my fully-loaded rifle deer, which I hugged close to his skinny frame. Warmth and affection radiated from my deadly gun. Slowly, I made my way to the bridge several blocks up the street. I staggered down the dirt embankment. Stumbling along the riverbank, I found a good hiding place among the weeds and brush. I sank to the ground like a dying elephant, and curled up in a pain-wracked ball.

The gurgle of the slow-moving stream and chattering of birds offered a momentary respite. But, nightmares surpassing all the terrifying reality of my early childhood kept me twitching and moaning through every moment of the endless night.

I awoke in the morning with my body swollen like one of those bloated war corpses I saw in the newsreels at the movies. Pain vibrated along every nerve. I was sure I couldn't stand up and walk, but I did. I made my way to school.

Completely wrapped in my sleeping bag, I was an object of curiosity, but not alarm. The first person I encountered in my homeroom was Mark. He made a grab for the barrel of the raised and aimed rifle, but I'd already applied enough pressure to the trigger. The .308 caliber slug traveled at 2300 feet-per-second when it left the muzzle, and Mark stood only four feet away. It went through the center of his face and was deflected downward and came out the back of his head and traveled on and took off the top of the head of the girl behind him. The slug then shattered the large glass window that took up half the wall past the dying girl and thudded in a pine tree twenty feet distant from the building before I heard the boom and felt the recoil. I ignored the screams of the students as I levered another round in the chamber and swung to my right to fire at the fleeing teacher. It was a wild shot, but the slug entered her body at shoulder level, went through her and continued on and pierced the wall behind her.

Like lava from an erupting volcano, a pool of crimson blood spread across the floor towards my feet. I didn't want that heavy, hot flow to stain my beloved black boots, so I quit shooting and walked out of the classroom.

I left the building and the school grounds and made my way back to the riverbank. Sirens filled the air as I stumbled along the narrow pathway looking for a hole that would allow me to crawl down to hell and burn forever. I tripped on a tree root and fell forward. When my face slammed into the ground, everything went black.

Holy shit! Jesus Christ! Goddamn! What horrible sin did I commit? Why have the sirens stopped? I lay in bed, my body vibrated and I dripped sweat.

I scanned my surroundings. I examined my undamaged body. Slowly, I realized it was all a horrific dream. Relief flooded through me.

I couldn't ever go back to sleep! I couldn't ever let that nightmare resume.

I must control my hate. I couldn't ever let that terrifying dream become the reality of my overwhelming desire for revenge. I had to get out of Utah.

CHAPTER FORTY-FOUR

U pon our return to Ogden, Utah, my oldest brother, Tommy, didn't show up to visit. Virginia expressed concern about him, so she and I made a short visit to his wife's poor, white-trash community. By then Diana had borne two of Tommy's children. She told us the sad story of how he had left the house one day to buy cigarettes and beer and didn't come home. Tommy deserted Diana and his two children exactly like our father abandoned Virginia, me and three of my brothers in Chicago when I was five-years-old.

Diana didn't invite us in. We stood outside the ragged, sagging screen-door as Virginia talked to her. We couldn't actually see Diana because she purposely hid in the darkest shadows of her hovel. Four-hundred and fifty-pounds is what she'd ballooned up to and she didn't want us to see what she'd become.

Her voice was still warm and friendly. One of her dirty, raggedy kids clung to Virginia. "Grandma, I love you," he chanted.

Virginia put her arms around the grimy little boy and pulled him close. "I love you too," she cooed.

Other dirty-faced children from the community crowded around looking for attention. It reminded me of a scene from a war movie where American G.I.'s were mobbed by the homeless waifs of Europe. Those raggedy and starving children begging for candy were the helpless victims of war. These children were the helpless victims of a society that couldn't or wouldn't help them escape from their cruel fate of being born in poverty and ignorance.

"If you hear from Tommy, please let me know," Diana's plaintive voice called from the shadows.

"Of course I will, Diana," Virginia replied in her most reassuring tone.

My mother gave her pitiful grandson a tearful goodbye hug.

I wanted to flee this terrible place as quickly as possible.

Soon after our visit with Diana, Virginia decided she was finished with Utah for good. She and I would move to California. A deeply-depressed Al Davey wasn't able to find any kind of work in Ogden. Never giving up on Virginia, he pleaded with her to let him drive us to the coast. Peggy refused to move again. She chose to stay behind in Ogden with friends. She wanted to finish high school in Utah.

Al, Virginia, and I packed his Ford to overflowing. Elation and depression flooded through me as we prepared for the familiar drive to Los Angeles. I wasn't sure if I'd ever see my lovely stepsister Peggy again. If I knew this was the end for her and me, just like a crystal glass hurled onto hard concrete, my heart would break in a thousand pieces. Peggy broke down and cried over the departure and loss of Virginia. She and my mother hugged tightly and said a tearful good bye to each other.

Peggy didn't embrace me, but she did say, "Goodbye Mickey." I recalled the last and longest conversation she and I had. "Mickey, you really don't appreciate what a wonderful mother you have!" she admonished me. As was my habit, I kept silent. I resolved to keep the story about my wretched years with Naomi to myself. Peggy didn't have a clue as to the truth about my mother. I was sure she didn't want to hear the horrific tales I could tell her.

It was 1957 and I careened up to sixteen-years-old. I was stuck inside the 1955 Ford Sedan with Al and Virginia and the merciless war she waged against him.

"I want to get out of Utah as quickly as possible," she said pointing to her map. "I hate this state. The Mormons are so prejudiced. Let's take Route 40 west to Nevada. We can then take Route 93 south to Las Vegas."

As we drove west, surrounded by a landscape of boring scrubland, Al attempted to break through her wall of silence.

"Are the air vents set the way you want them?"

"It's just too hot here. Nothing is going to feel good until we reach the ocean breezes," she grumbled.

"How are you doing back there, Mickey?" Al looked at me in the rear-view mirror.

With so many of our personal possessions stuffed in the back seat, I barely had room to wiggle. "I'm fine, Al." If he thought his kindness to me might soften her attitude towards him, he was wrong. It never did.

I hated the atmosphere inside the vehicle, but every mile of highway passing under our wheels and separating us further from Ogden and the Mormons made me more hopeful about my future. Our route was mostly through desolation. When we finally crossed the state line into Nevada at Wendover, the heavy load of Mormon condemnation and oppression lifted from my shoulders. I hoped I wouldn't ever set foot in the hellish state of Utah again.

Virginia let out a big sigh. "I'm so glad to leave Utah," she said. "I'll never come back here."

Traveling the narrow, two-lane blacktop Route 93 south from Wendover to Las Vegas would bore most people to oblivion. Despite the heat, dust, and endless mirages, I saw a refuge in the barrenness of the desert. I tried to imagine living the life of a desert lizard.

Far away from the road and noise and litter, I sat in the shade of a large rock. I waited for a delicious bug to wander within range of my tongue. The sounds in my desert world were always restrained. Soft, warm breezes carried the soothing scents of soil and greenery to me. Sudden showers of clean rain brought millions of aromatic wildflowers to life. I knew the location of every cool, bubbling spring. I roamed my paradise cautiously, always alert for predators, but I was free and happy.

A semi-truck barred down the road and brought me back to reality. When we passed those smoke-spewing, eighteen-wheeler behemoths traveling in the opposite direction, our vehicle shuddered from bumper to bumper.

Our nighttime arrival in sparkling Las Vegas brought us back to the more familiar route we traveled just a couple of years ago to Los Angeles. There were more casinos, hotels, and gamblers. The cascading and blinking lights of the gambling palaces along the strip couldn't put a thaw in the barrier Virginia built between her and Al.

"Would you like to stop and play the slot machines, Virginia?" Al cajoled.

"No, Al! We aren't on a vacation," she reminded him impatiently.

We traveled through the remainder of the always brightly-lit and active city in silence.

I remembered I stood next to Peggy on the sidewalk outside the flashy Flamingo casino. We spent many hours together in the back seat of the old Pontiac. Now, I was alone in the back seat of the Ford. How much aloneness waited in my future?

Al slept in the car as she and I shared a seedy motel room near a noisy truck stop just outside the city limits. We made a bed for me on the floor. I was exhausted enough to sleep soundly. The electric tension that always prevailed when Virginia and Al were within sight of each other was gone. Noisy trucks arriving and departing throughout the night barely disturbed me.

In the morning, Al looked like a dried-up, desert discard. His appearance deepened her disgust and incited her abuse.

"You look terrible, Al," she exclaimed. "And you smell like a nasty old dog."

"I'm sorry, Virginia. I'll clean up if you let me use the room."

"Please do. Mickey and I are going to breakfast by ourselves."

His face sagged even more. He looked like a sick old-man facing his last days on earth. As usual, I felt sorry for him. Actually, I felt more sympathy for him than I ever felt for myself.

She and I walked to the nearby diner for breakfast. It was only a short stack for me, but I piled on lots of butter and maple syrup. She drank black coffee and consumed an order of toast and smoked cigarettes. Thankfully, Al didn't show up and make an embarrassing attempt to join us.

Crowded back in the overloaded car, we continued our southwest journey to the Promised Land. The bleak drive to Barstow would bring us to our connection point with Route 66. We sped past other people's shattered dreams littering the roadside. The sight of broken-down automobiles and abandoned mobile homes gathering rust made me appreciate that our auto kept running, and guaranteed the continued success of my flight to freedom and a better life. I longed for our destination of wide sandy beaches and the vast Pacific Ocean.

CHAPTER FORTY-FIVE

Our arrival in sprawling, congested Los Angeles by way of Route 66 was on a warm day with a bright sun attempting to break through the smoggy haze. We passed oil drilling derricks and working oil rigs, which always fascinated me. Hundreds of rigs that looked like prehistoric beasts were pumping without pause as they sucked oil out of the earth. I imagined owning a house here and discovering oil in my back-yard. I became a millionaire driving luxurious cars and turned my little house into a grand, spacious mansion.

Weaving our way up to Hollywood and driving along crowded Sunset Boulevard brought classic movie scenes I viewed in dark theatres to vivid life. Virginia made it clear she wanted to live in the city of Hollywood itself. No questions or suggestions for an alternative would be tolerated.

She scanned the local newspaper she bought.

"Here's a possible, Al." She told him the address and barked driving instructions to him. "Don't get us lost now."

We located the classic, single-story, pink-stucco apartment

complex with a walkway and small green lawns dividing its two rows of abodes. From the outside the place looked decent. It fit perfectly in the movie version of quaint living quarters for a glamorous, aspiring movie actress with a limited budget.

"We'll call the manager in the morning. Let's find a decent place to spend the night."

Daylight faded fast as we searched and only found a seedy motel that had to suffice.

"God, I'm tired of staying in such dumps," Virginia complained bitterly. "I think prostitutes are working out of here."

"Maybe the apartment we drove by will be nice," Al offered.

"I hope so."

After we carried in our luggage, we settled in our garishly wallpapered room. Despite how diligently I looked, I didn't spot any women who were recognizable as whores. I'd hoped to see a few wandering the premises with their customers following them.

"Al, you and Mickey can make beds on the floor." Al knew better than to complain.

She gave me a smile. "I slept on hard floors many times when I was young like you, Mickey." She offered me a hug and I limply accepted it. Al reached out a hand to touch her on her shoulder, but she dodged his effort and gave him a murderous look.

The following morning, we met with the manager of the apartment building. We rented a small courtyard flat located close to Sunset Boulevard. She had the bedroom. Al was consigned to the couch. Again, I had to sleep on the floor. Al was denied any entry to the bedroom.

. . .

The next day, Virginia found a job as a waitress at a small diner on Sunset Boulevard. The greasy spoon was open for breakfast and lunch only. The good-natured Greek owner, who looked classic Mr. Hollywood with his deep tan and flashy fake-gold neck-chain, offered me a job of cleaning up after business hours. My work time would fit perfectly with a school schedule. I was disappointed there wasn't any Hollywood glamour to my new work, but at least it paid. It wasn't much, but it included one free meal and I could eat a lot in one sitting.

Al wandered the streets of Hollywood looking for a meaningful job that didn't exist.

The colorful neighborhood, with lots of palm trees and sculptured Mediterranean architecture, was exactly like the Hollywood I saw in the movies. Warm-pastel-colored houses with red tile roofs filled the hillsides around me. Looking up past the exotic palm trees, I saw the famous sign perched just below the top of one of the highest hills. It spelled out "Hollywood" in giant white letters. I loved the change from the sterile, gray, desert drabness of Utah.

I strolled along Sunset Boulevard like I was a long-time local. I walked over to Hollywood Boulevard to visit Grauman's Chinese Theatre. I studied the hand and foot imprints of the world-famous movie stars pressed in the sidewalk for all of eternity. Like many others, I placed my hands and feet in those concrete impressions. I couldn't find a perfect fit. I guess that meant I wouldn't ever be among the elite who filled the giant movie screens of the world's posh theaters. Mostly harmless and noisy tourists crowded around the exotically-elaborate Grauman's Chinese Theater. I was safe in this colorful new world. Then, a slithery, reptilian man who lurked at the edge of the throng stared at me. Damn. I needed to be as alert for sexual predators here as in Chicago.

I enrolled at nearby Hollywood High School. What a strange place. Most of the students stayed aloof. They trod the hallways like aliens. The classroom atmosphere was as subdued as the services at a funeral home. Nobody paid any attention to me. They barely paid attention to each other. Some gathered in small groups of people that looked like carbon copies of themselves. It seemed I was invisible to these sun-tanned Californians. That was fine with me. I appreciated being ignored. I liked living in my own private world.

I wore my black leather jacket, Levi's, and black engineer boots. I wasn't a hood like the tough guy that picked on James Dean in the movie, "Rebel Without a Cause." I didn't want to be involved in any rumbles and have someone pull a switchblade on me. I didn't have a hot rod for chicken races and I didn't have a pretty girl hanging on my arm. Maybe that was good. A guy can get beat up by thugs if he tries to defend a pretty girl's honor. I stayed silent and kept to myself. The teachers at school did voice my name during roll call, so I knew I was a real, live human.

Al couldn't find work. He hated Hollywood and he missed Peggy.

"You might as well go back to Utah, Al," Virginia chided him. "You'll never fit in here. You're a country boy. California is too sophisticated for you."

He finally gave up on my mother. He said his tearful goodbyes. He probably hoped she'd declare she'd been terribly wrong and embrace him and ask him to stay with her forever.

No fucking way. This was Hollywood, but there wasn't going to be a happy movie ending to their relationship. She wished him a good future, but didn't offer any smiles or warmth.

CHAPTER FORTY-SIX

I attended Hollywood High School, my third school during my sophomore year, and cleaned the diner in the evenings. Virginia did her waitress work and she and I even went to the movies together a few times. If this calm lasted a couple of years, I'd reach my all-important goal of finishing high school. That'd be the end of schooling for me. I'd work at a good job and wouldn't depend on anyone for a place to live and food to eat. I'd move on with my life. There was hope for me.

In my free time, I checked out the Hollywood movie studios still in business. Twentieth Century Fox, Columbia, and Paramount were active, but the RKO lot was out of business and being dismantled. I couldn't gain entry to any of the famous, fantasy factories for a tour, but I observed what I could through barred gates, and I peered over high walls to see the tops of the movie sets.

I made my way up to Griffith Park. I did a quick walk-through of the impressive interior of the Observatory. Outside, I stood where James Dean was filmed having a switchblade fight with the local bully. The lookout point provided a perfect view of the top of the thick layer of smog blanketing Los Angeles. I walked around Griffith Park, but I grew weary of the place and of avoiding predators. Being a solitary kid on the streets can become terribly depressing. I headed back down to town.

A group of plumbers from a nearby shop were regular customers at the diner where Virginia and I worked. One of them was immediately interested in Virginia. He aggressively courted her and soon, he visited our apartment regularly.

Hank Brawl was a cigar smoking, whiskey swilling, loud-mouthed, navy veteran of World War Two. He bragged loudly about being a former amateur boxer. He called himself "the little man on the hill." He stood only five-foot five-inches tall and I'd grown to five-foot eleven-inches and a scrawny 135 pounds. I immediately became the target of his verbal harassment.

"Jesus," Hank said. "You're so skinny, Mickey."

"Yeah," I agreed. I ate lots of good, free food at the diner, but it never showed on me.

"Do you have a girlfriend?"

"Not right now." The bastard was slowly moving in the apartment Virginia and I shared. He desperately wanted me completely erased from the picture.

"You need to lift weights, kid. Put some muscle on your skinny body."

"Sure." He was pushing me towards the door.

"Why don't you leave him alone, Hank?" Virginia protested. Her voice sounded like she really meant to defend me.

"I'm just trying to help him, Virginia. He's too damn skinny. He sure does eat a lot though."

It wasn't any of his fucking business how much I ate. He didn't pay for our food. She and I bought our own groceries. He only brought by the apartment what he wanted to eat.

I really despised him. He had a doughy face and carried a paunch around his middle. His teeth were yellowed from smoking his stinking cigars. He loved salami sandwiches. His breath was foul and I had to turn my face away when he crowded me. What did Virginia see in him? Maybe it was all about him being blustery to compliment and impress her. She always fell for the superficial, bullshit artists. Sadly, except for Al Davey, that's the kind of man she always attached herself to.

It certainly was true I didn't smile much. I was too serious. I was too sensitive. I couldn't pretend to be pleased when I was obligated to spend time around an asshole like Hank Brawl.

"I was lightweight champion on my ship during the war. I wasn't tall, but I was tough. I kicked all those tall guy's asses."

"That's good, Hank."

Hank liked to spar at me to show off his quick moves. I never raised my hands. I knew the opportunity he was looking for. He wanted to land a solid, open-handed slap to my face, to humiliate me in front of Virginia. He really wanted to humble me and his nasty words by themselves weren't accomplishing his goal.

Chewing on his soggy cigar, he sparred at my face. He was quick of hand. I believed his fists could do serious damage to me. I sat unmoving on the couch as he bounced about in his boxer stance and punched closer and closer to my face. I felt air movement as his open hands flashed by my eyes. I watched him, but I kept my arms crossed. He paused and glared at me and chomped on his soggy cigar. I saw boiling frustration on his ugly face.

"The men who fought in World War Two were real men," he declared.

"Yeah, I'm sure they were."

"You wouldn't have made it in that military."

"You're right, Hank."

He puffed deeply on his cigar. He blew a cloud of cigar smoke directly in my face.

"You should have seen the battle of Midway. What a show. Those Jap kamikaze planes filled the sky." He picked bits of soggy cigar tobacco from his teeth and lips. "We blasted dozens of those yellow bastards out of the sky. Those crazy Nips kept coming."

Hank constantly complained about Jews and why they let themselves be victims in the Holocaust. He did admit there'd been a few good Jewish boxers. Often he said, "Goddamn, I hate Jews." I heard plenty of this kind of talk growing up and couldn't understand hating a person you didn't personally know. Of course, many Mormons hated me because I wasn't a member of their religion. Many people also hated Catholics and I grew up Catholic and had my first communion. Recently, I walked away from all religion and swore to never enter a church again. I didn't pray to the invisible God either.

I gave up my fantasy of Virginia and me rebuilding a life together. I minimized my time at the apartment to avoid Hank Brawl's constant posturing and never-ceasing bullying.

I liked to visit Graumann's Chinese theatre. The lobby was graced with large expanses of colorfully-veined marble columns and floors. Elegantly-curving, thickly-carpeted, wide staircases ascended to the balcony entrances. Rich-red colored, floor-to-ceiling drapery covered the soaring auditorium walls. I sat in that immense and ornate movie palace to watch "The Bridge on the River Kwai." I watched as even the biggest and bravest of warriors suffered abuse. The mightiest could be killed by a single bullet to the brain. Many of the toughest soldiers in the film were scrawny like me. I related to them. Hank Brawl didn't know what the hell he was talking about.

Crowded theatres were good because I didn't have to worry about the men who slithered down the aisles and sat in the row directly behind me. When the Chinese theatre was nearly empty during a feature film, it was a troublesome place. So were most of the other cinemas in Hollywood. Predators always lurked close by. They fiddled with their clothes. Their breathing was always heavy with lust. The boldest leaned forward to whisper close to my ear. Many a time, I wished I carried a thick, wooden ax-handle in my hand. I'd spin around and smash their ugly faces to a pulp. Even better, I imagined being a Samurai Warrior. I'd be armed with a razor-sharp samurai sword. With one swing, I'd slice off the predator's ugly heads. With one kick, I'd send blood-spewing, predator heads bouncing down the main aisles of the theatres.

My older brother Ben visited Virginia and me a number of times. My youngest brother, John, came along with him on a couple of those visits. Ben got along with Hank. They shared a love of loud talk and bullying bluster. Ben was willing to spar with Hank and suffer a few hard slaps to his face. That put Hank Brawl in heaven. Of course, if Ben lived in the same apartment with the bully Hank, it'd be a much different story.

Ben bragged about how much fun it was living in Lawndale with our father. He went on about what a blast the pool parties were. He suggested I forgive Orin for his abandonment and years of neglect. I should come by for a visit and have a happy reunion with my asshole of a father.

Virginia asked me if I wanted to visit my supposed father. I hadn't seen Orin since 1947. It was eleven years since he'd walked out, taken my baby brother with him, and abandoned our family in Chicago. He never sent one penny of support for the four sons he left behind. He never communicated with any of us. He'd been completely missing during my four years of slavery to the monster, Naomi. To him, I was nothing. Was he really my father? He always called me 'Blondie" and claimed I wasn't his kid. My only memory of him was fear and nightmares. My oldest brother, Tommy, told me Orin believed me to be a bastard. Tommy himself believed me to be a bastard. Everyone in that branch of my family liked to joke about me being the milkman's kid. I never asked Virginia what the real truth was.

How could I pass up such a momentous occasion as a family reunion? How would I address a man whose name was on my birth certificate as being my father, but who always made jokes about me resembling random strangers? The word "Daddy" didn't pop into my mind.

"Hey," Hank said. "It might be a good idea for you to live with your father, Mickey. You'd be around your brothers all the time."

"I wasn't really thinking of Mickey moving away," Virginia said. "We'd just go out to Lawndale for a visit."

"I don't think he'd want me living with him and his new family," I said. I wondered if "Daddy" wasn't still the monster who taunted me when I was a helpless baby, toddler, and little boy.

"Call his father and see how he feels about Mickey living with him, Virginia," Hank Brawl enthused.

"Well, if Mickey really wants to," she turned and smiled at me. "I would miss you so much though, honey."

Oh yeah. Fucking right, she'd miss me. She had Hank Brawl and also owned a black poodle dog. She acted like the sun rose and set every day on the silly little yapper's ass. At least curly-haired Mimi satisfied her need to love something she thought loved her back. She leaned over and gave me a hug. I let her put her arms around me, but like always, I didn't respond. My mother would miss me? What a joke. She sure as hell hadn't hesitated about leaving me with Rose and George for a year and then with the monster Naomi for four brutal years. I really didn't have a strong desire to know the terrible truth about anything. Accepting and living with the many lies making up my life was fine with me.

CHAPTER FORTY-SEVEN

L awndale was fifteen miles due south of Hollywood by
way of La Brea Ave.

Hank drove his tinny, piece of crap, German-made Borg-
ward Isabella automobile as if he was the mightiest king of the
road. We kept the windows rolled down so his constant puffs of
cigar smoke could escape from the tiny vehicle. Cramped in the
small back seat of that piece of junk, my eyes suffered from
both his stinking, stogie exhalations and from the thick, Los
Angeles smog we drove through.

"Yes sir, Mick. This is going to be a great move for you to
live with your father." In the rear-view mirror, Hank gave me
one of his smuggest looks. He picked a piece of soggy tobacco
from his yellowed teeth. "It's too crowded for the three of us in
that little apartment."

What a fucking asshole, I thought. It'd been Virginia and
my place before he crowded his way in our lives.

"Let's see how he feels about it after he talks to his father,"
Virginia said. She turned in her seat and smiled back at me.

"He really needs to make this move," Hank grumbled.

I hadn't seen my father for eleven years. How the hell did I know what was going to happen? For sure, I needed to get away from Hank Brawl and his constant harassment.

We passed Los Angeles International Airport within a couple of hundred feet of the beginning of one of its busiest runways. Huge planes roared over the top of us as they readied to touch down. Those noisy jets drowned out Hank's harping for a few moments.

"This would be a perfect move for you Mick," he shouted.

What the hell. Maybe "Dad" reconsidered. Maybe he didn't really believe I was a bastard. Maybe, with age, he'd become a decent human being. Maybe, this would be the warm and loving home I always searched for. I leaned back in my seat and closed my eyes. I struggled to remember my early years in Chicago with my mother, my supposed father, and my brothers.

I remembered. I remembered what my supposed father was like.

Chicago, Illinois. February, 1946. Whenever Daddy was unemployed, Mommy worked longer hours as a waitress and he stayed home and looked after us, his five sons. He sat at the kitchen table, sipped from a cup of coffee and puffed on Camel cigarettes. When he was bored, Daddy liked to play fight with us.

"Come on, boys." He stuck his chin out and pointed to it with one finger. "Let's see if any of you boys can hit me right there." He tapped his finger against his chin.

"I'm not afraid," Tommy yelled. Arms swinging wildly, Tommy charged. Daddy easily held my oldest brother away with a hand to Tommy's forehead. He laughed at Tommy's futile efforts and after a few more wild swings, Daddy hit him on his cheek with a flat hand. The slap made a loud sound, left a red mark, and raised Tommy's fury.

"I'll help you, Tommy," Ben said as he rushed forward and

swung wildly at Daddy. Daddy easily held Tommy and Ben at arm's length and laughed at their frustration.

"Help us, Mickey," Ben yelled.

Daddy glanced over at me and sneered. "Yeah, Blondie," he mocked. "Come over here and hit me."

I hated Daddy when he called me Blondie. I wanted to hit him, but was too afraid of him to rush into the battle.

"Come on and help us, Mickey," Ben yelled louder.

Daddy hit Ben with a hard slap to his face.

Ben staggered backwards and put his hand up to his cheek. Tears welled up in his eyes and then burst forth in a flood.

"That hurt, Daddy," Ben sobbed.

"That hurt," Daddy mimicked Ben. "Ben's a big crybaby."

"That's not fair, Daddy," Ben sobbed.

"Boo hoo," Daddy mimicked. "That's not fair, Daddy."

"Quit being a crybaby, Ben," Tommy yelled. My oldest brother hated it when Ben and I were weak.

"Boo hoo," Daddy mimicked louder. "Ben is such a sissy. Ben is such a crybaby."

Ben hated being called "crybaby." More tears boiled up in his eyes.

"Don't you other boys be a big crybaby like Ben," Daddy said. "Boo hoo. Even Blondie doesn't cry that much."

"Why didn't you help us, Mickey?" Tommy glared at me.

"Yeah, Blondie," Daddy taunted me again. "Come on over. You know you want to hit me really hard."

Overcome with fear and shame, I stayed back. I really wanted to join the battle and hit Daddy and maybe kill him, but I knew I'd cry when he slapped my face. He'd make fun of me worse than he did Ben. I never wanted to do things that made Daddy notice me.

My younger brother, Steve, didn't like to be a part of the play *fighting. Luckily for him, he was too young for Daddy to slap him hard on his face.*

Tommy didn't cry anymore when Daddy hit him. He got angrier and fought back with more ferocity. I think he wanted to kill Daddy almost as much as I did.

Ben always hoped he'd come out a winner over Daddy and Daddy would praise him for being tough. His biggest hope was Daddy would say he loved him. He always charged into the melee, flailed away with his hardest fists, and gave the play fight his all. Daddy easily held him at a distance, laughed at him, and always got in the hard slap to Ben's face. Ben didn't understand he wouldn't ever win.

I figured out Daddy's game real quick. A couple of hard slaps to my face was all I needed to understand Daddy would always win, and I'd always be a crying loser.

Deep inside of me, I prayed Daddy would die. He'd die just like the bad men in the movies. The good and brave cowboys would shoot him to death. Even better, the good cowboys would put a noose around Daddy's neck and hang him from the strongest branch of a big tree. Daddy would swing from the tree branch forever. Never again would he make jokes about me being the milkman's kid.

I was sure Daddy didn't just dislike me. He hated me...

CHAPTER FORTY-EIGHT

"We're here, Mickey." Virginia's voice startled me out of my reverie.

We pulled up in front of my possible new residence. Ben and John waited. A strange man stood behind them. We parked and climbed out of the car. A happy Ben surged forward and hugged Virginia. He then clasped me in a hug and said, "I'm really glad you're home, little bother." I now stood two inches taller than him, but he still liked to call me, "little brother." I sensed he wasn't crazy about the new reality of my being taller than him.

Baby brother John hugged Virginia like he was fulfilling a duty he really didn't understand. He accepted her "I've never been so happy in my entire life" hugs like he had on his visits to Hollywood. He shook my hand. The brotherly bond between him and I was growing with each meeting. Hank Brawl chomped on his soggy cigar. He started strutting as soon as he exited his cheap, little car. The strange man who was supposed to be my father looked like he wanted to out-strut Hank. Even though the strange man was a couple of inches taller and more handsome than Hank, he was the loser this day. He didn't have Virginia. She looked shapely, attractive, and sported a confident smile. The strange man hugged Virginia too warmly. Hank hopped about like a jealous rooster guarding one of its hens.

The strange man looked me up and down with doubt. Then he spread his arms open to offer an obligatory hug. I hesitated a moment. I sized him up.

He was thirty-nine years old. His dark, receding hair was slicked back. He stood several inches shorter than me. He was cleanly shaved, with a neatly trimmed mustache and a protruding, soft belly. He wore pleasantly scented cologne and a practiced, phony smile.

Then, I remembered who he was. Vivid memories of his cruelty when I was a small, helpless child came to me. I finally accepted his embrace. I hated the physical contact with him. The demon inside me raged against my hypocrisy. I pushed back against the demon. I didn't allow little Mickey to come to the surface and scream his hate. I didn't feel any sense of kinship or any kind of human connection with this slick character who embraced me without any warmth. Seeing and having physical contact with him sickened me. He was just another monster. I quickly decided the bastard couldn't really be my father.

Truth slapped me in the face. Shit. I still didn't have a father. Virginia planned to leave me in the hands of this slimy stranger. I'd begun to expect better from her. Goddamn. When would I quit being such a stupid fool?

Ben was the only one of the greeting party who smiled sincerely and welcomed me with open arms. John didn't really understand the situation.

"The high school here is real friendly, Mick," Ben said. "The kids aren't at all like those Mormons back in Utah or those stuck-up snobs in Hollywood."

During this minor celebration over my visit, we talked about the possibility of my moving in the room off the garage and bunking with Ben. Ben endorsed the idea with his usual overwrought enthusiasm.

"I hope you move in with me, little brother." He punched me on the arm. He was looking forward to wrestling matches.

"We're really crowded here, but I guess we can find room for you, Mickey," my supposed father reluctantly agreed. The cowardly bastard hadn't yet worked up the guts to call me "Blondie."

Hank gushed with happiness at the idea of getting rid of me. I didn't really have a choice. I had to get away from Hank Brawl. I desperately wanted to finish high school. My goals were modest. I needed at least that minimal education to have any hope of surviving in the treacherous world surrounding me. The bizarre conditions of my life threatened to pull me down in a black pit of failure. I was slogging through merciless quicksand and needed to grasp at any possibility of a helping hand.

I'd have much better luck with my mother if I'd been born a poodle dog. She valued her dogs highly. I knew Virginia didn't ever want to have a conversation about her abandonments of me and my brothers. She didn't ever want to know the truth of my life with Naomi. She'd hate and disown me if I ever told her the details of my hellish four years of slavery and beatings. I knew she didn't need my presence to make her life complete. She could always find someone to love her. I didn't have that luxury. I didn't have anyone else. It was impossibly difficult for me to attach to people. I could continue to enjoy my mother's conditional love, as long as I kept my mouth shut.

I understood and accepted my status as an outsider in my mother's and my supposed father's families. Like a ragged hitchhiker who wandered in off the heartless road, I grasped at any pittance offered to me.

I saw hope, though. Surely, a terrible mistake occurred when I was born. I really belonged to a loving, intelligent, and wealthy family. The hospital fucked up and put the stupid Shafer kid in my bassinet. That low-life charlatan was living with my real parents and enjoying the wonderful life that was supposed to be mine.

I didn't expect much from my supposed father. He wouldn't ever change. I was sure he'd continue his brutal taunting of me he'd enjoyed so much during my first five years of existence. He was evil and ignorant to his core. He'd harass me because it was his nature. But, I no longer feared him. I'd find many small moments and methods to reap revenge. I was older. I would survive. Damn.

ACKNOWLEDGMENT

Cyndy, Robert M. Shafer's daughter

Robert M. Shafer passed away in August 2020. He would have wanted Lisa Kastner with Running Wild Press to be acknowledged, for being willing to publish this book after his passing.

Running Wild Press publishes stories that cross genres with great stories and writing. RIZE publishes great genre stories written by people of color and by authors who identify with other marginalized groups. Our team consists of:

Lisa Diane Kastner, Founder and Executive Editor
Cody Sisco, Acquisitions Editor, RIZE
Benjamin White, Acquisition Editor, Running Wild
Peter A. Wright, Acquisition Editor, Running Wild
Resa Alboher, Editor
Angela Andrews, Editor
Sandra Bush, Editor
Ashley Crantas, Editor
Rebecca Dimyan, Editor
Abigail Efird, Editor
Aimee Hardy, Editor
Henry L. Herz, Editor
Cecilia Kennedy, Editor
Barbara Lockwood, Editor
Scott Schultz, Editor

Evangeline Estropia, Product Manager
Kimberly Ligutan, Product Manager
Lara Macaione, Marketing Director
Joelle Mitchell, Licensing and Strategy Lead
Pulp Art Studios, Cover Design
Standout Books, Interior Design
Polgarus Studios, Interior Design

Learn more about us and our stories at www. runningwildpress.com

Loved this story and want more? Follow us at www.runningwildpress.com, www.facebook.com/runningwildpress, on Twitter @lisadkastner @RunWildBooks